Something Else Yearbook, 1974

Something Else Yearbook

1974
Something Else Press, Inc.
Barton   **Brownington**   **Berlin**

Editor: Jan Herman

L. C. Catalog Card No.: 72-90050

ISBN: 0-87110-091-6

Manufactured in the United States of America

Contents

SINE NOMINE

Tell the audience that they are going to hear a piece of music,
and ask them to choose between the following three pieces:

1. Adagio - Andante Allegretto - Allegro

2. Adagio - Allegro - Adagio - Presto

3. Allegro - Presto - Andante - Allegro

Tell the audience that if some of the pieces are going to get the
same number of votes, they will both (or all three) be played. If
none of the pieces are going to get votes, they will all be played.

Ask then the audience to vote.

> (they can cry)
> (they can put up their fingers)
> (they can write on a piece of paper)
> (etc.)

Play the winning piece on a metronome.

Adagio =   72
Andante =   92
Allegretto =   120
Allegro =   144
Presto =   192

Each Movement: 2 minutes

AN ADDITION TO SINE NOMINE

The metronome has to be played in such a way that the audience can
only see it, but NOT HEAR IT.

Opus 21:

Perform something at intervals for a long time.

> (version to the "SUMMEREXHIBITION L":
> Ligeti: "Trois Bagatelles"
> intervals: a half an hour
> from 14.00 o'clock to 21.00 o'clock)

Opus 24:

Sit down during December 11, 1969 from 7 PM to
8.03 PM (danish time) and think about the people
over the whole world, who may be performing this
composition.

Opus 28:

Run around like a half-castrated reindeer.

Opus 29:

1. Select some objects, which address themselves
   to your acoustic imagination.

2. Play with the objects after a predetermined system.

Opus 34:

To call my compositions by Opus and a number.

Opus 36:

Write two exactly identical envelopes to me and place
with tape the right amount in coins instead of stamps.
The put the one into the other and send the letter to
me. If I get the letter I will maybe be able to see the
exact difference between these two envelopes, and, maybe
I will have a useful relationship. And maybe I will be
a clever boy. And I will be a happy boy.

adapted to the performer(s) at stage

! when the performance starts you will find on the stage and around in the room !
! a number of objects + one circle   !

¶ choose one or more than one object and place it in the circle or let it stay   ¶
¶ wherever you will find it   ¶

! you can work as a single person - you can work as a member of a group -   !
! you can work as a member of the whole audience - please consider these   !
! possibilities   !

DEAL WITH THE CHOSEN OBJECT(S) IN THE FOLLOWING WAY:::::::::::::::::::

Create five different actions to be performed with the object but without
realizing any of them

1.: has to follow : a way of creation which is developing inside a well defined
    viewpoint confirming this and without adding some eidetically new aspects to it
2.: has to follow a way of creation which is developing from a more or less
    definite viewpoint but following a well defined kind of moving
3.: has to follow : a way of creation which is developing from a more or less
    definite viewpoint and ending in a well defined new viewpoint
4.: has to follow : a way of creation which is not moving and which is independent
    of any origins
5.: has to follow : the unconsionously depended spontaneity

then select and realize one of the actions

----

you will probably get a number of copies of these instructions
if you do so : please distribute them to your best friends after the performance

----

! definition : welldefinated (viewpoint or moving) : only depended on totally   !
!   controllable activities   !

4 Versions of Opus 47

Opus 47:

Material necessary for Opus 47 should be used.

Opus 47:

Make a remark (i.e. explanation, analysis etc.) to an object using for the reason of documentation and communication abstracts from the object in a way relevant to the method.

Opus 47:

Each performer is equipped with a microphone - the microphones are connected with one or some (as you like) loudspeaker(s). The performers are performing (playing, not-playing, acting, not-acting, speaking, not-speaking, dancing, not-dancing etc. etc.).

Everytime a performer has discovered some conventions, forms, ideas etc. etc., has some informal associations, formal associations, impulses etc. etc. in and/or by his and/or the other performers performing, he tells the microphone.

Opus 47:

Opus 38:

/ the interlude of "We're Gonna Be In" _____
    piano

pause   / "Her Bathing Suit Never Got Wet" _____
        piano

pause   / I regret the bad circumstances for recording _____
        voice

Play the piano in a quick, lazy way - Talk with a sober voice.

Opera 25

Divide the audience into flexible and variable groups and
<u>ask</u> the groups to perform group-actions with definite durations.

Let the single group perform the single action coincident with
the other groups.

Let the single group change between several different actions.

It is permitted to let a group and/or the groups repeat some of
the actions (or them all).

The actions have to be developed according to: the disposition
and the faculty and the milieu and the conception and the
composition of the audience.

And you have to create the single action and the relationship
between the actions by a way of creation

     which is independent of any origins and not moving (Kalpa).

or a way of creation which is as close as possible to this
paragraph.

THREE UNTITLED POEMS

for Dick Wold

6

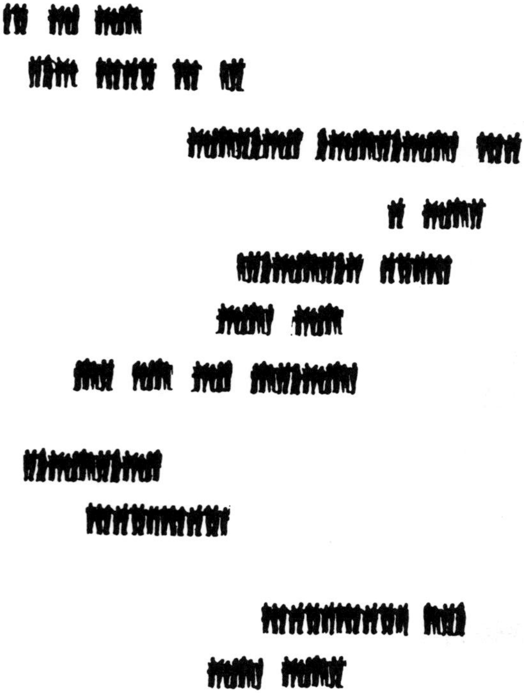

8

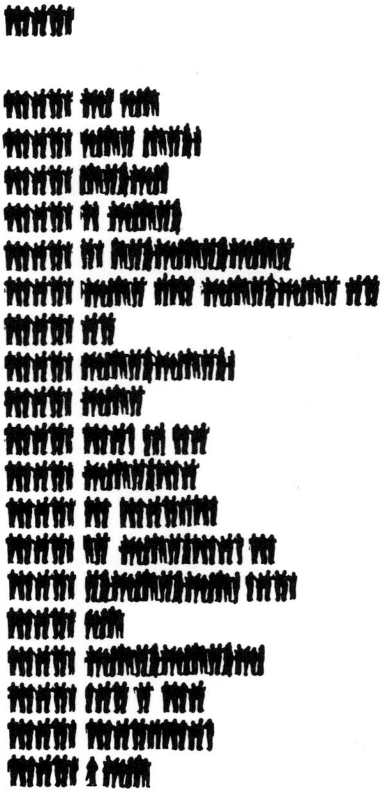

Paul-Armand Gette is neither a scientist nor an artist. His work includes all categories and classifications. What interests him most of all are the commonest natural phenomena, ordinary plants, the habitats of certain insects, the most banal and frequented territories: a vague piece of ground, the banks of a river in a big town.

At the start, his attitude is a sort of dream in the sense that Bachelard defined. He lets himself be guided by things according to how they catch his attention: here he picks up a dead branch, turns up a stone, examines a plant. It is at this first stage that he chooses the areas where he will apply his methods of "reading": a parcel of ground, a series of plants, a family of insects...

At a second stage, he makes a more or less partial description of the chosen elements. Sometimes a list of names suffices, or a simple casting, or a string of figures. Sometimes several approaches complement each other for the study of a single element' (plant, photograph, card, diagram.)

At the last stage, which is the presentation of the work, the documents are reorganized according to his general intuition, the subjective vision: such and such an element is eliminated in favor of another, such and such an indication is added, etc.

In using the clear and exact language of scientific disciplines, Gette rediscovers the imprecision, vagueness and haze of the intuition. For the manifold phenomena of nature are irreducible to any one language, be it the most rational and the most informative. By multiplying points of view, Gette manages to suggest the complexity and the diversity of the most commonplace landscape.

Certain elements of the description arouse memories in us while others confront us with a profusion that we did not imagine. In order to understand, it is not necessary to decipher the scientific code used. For Paul-Armand Gette does not aim at a logical explanation of natural phenomena: his aim is not to say why there is such and such a species here and another elsewhere.

He deflects scientific language from its habitual use in order to practice a kind of education in perception. He uses the most abstract possible means to.plunge us into a concrete universe. He upsets our perceptual habits and invites us to refashion for ourselves the very experience of perception.

---Bernard Borgeaud
(trans. by Jonathan Benthall)

This text is to be run with Gotte's photos.

Ringsjön (Sweden). Scirpus lacustris L.   august 1971

Fauna (coleoptera carabidae) :

        Bembidium (Peryphus) tetracolum Say.
        Pterostichus (s. str.) nigrita F.
        Pterostichus (s. str.) strenuus Panz.
        Agonum (s. str.) marginatum L.

Flora :

                                                                  79%

        Polygonum amphibium L.
        Lysimachia vulgaris L.
        Scirpus lacustris L.
        Calamagrostis lanceolata Roth.

11

Brighton (Black Rock). Matthiola incana Br.   september 1972

Flora(overcliff) :

            Matthiola incana Br.
            Diplotaxis muralis DC.
            Lepidium draba L.
            Spergularia salina J. & C. Presl.
            Trifolium fragiferum L.
            Helminthia echioides Gaertn.
            Plantago coronopus L.
            Beta maritima L.
            Atriplex latifolia Wahl. var. salina
            Agropyrum pungens Roem. & S.
            Bromus sterilis L.
            Festuca ovina L.

Paris. Tussilago farfara L.   april 1972

Flora (the right bank of the Seine) :

> Sagina procumbens L.
> Tussilago farfara L.
> Taraxacum officinale Wiggers
> Sonchus asper All.
> Scrofularia nodosa L.
> Mentha aquatica L.
> Lycopus europaeus L.
> Rumex hydrolapathum Huds.
> Ficus carica L.
> Carpinus betulus L.
> Salix aurita L.
> Salix caprea L.
> Salix fragilis L.
> Salix alba L.
> Populus nigra L.
> Platanus vulgaris Spach.
> Alnus glutinosa Gaertn.
> Juncus glaucus Ehrh.
> Juncus bufonius L.
> Carex leporina L.

London (Hammersmith). Salix alba L.   august 1972

Flora (East bank of the Thames) :

     Ranunculus sceleratus L.
     Roripa amphibia Bess.
     Sorbus aria Crantz.
     Lythrum salicaria L.
     Heracleum spondylium L.
     Artemisia vulgaris L.
     Veronica anagallis aquatica L.
     Fraxinus exelsior L.
     Salix alba L.
     Populus nigra L.
     Lycopus europaeus L.
     Rumex sangineus L.
     Juncus glaucus Ehrh.
     Juncus articulatus L.
     Juncus bufonius L.
     Bromus asper Murr.

The Something Else Gallery invites you to attend

The inauguration of **Wolf Vostell's T.O.T.,** to **begin** at **midnight** on the night of **August 20/21st, 1972,** and to end at midnight twenty four hours later. The T.O.T., is in Barton, Vermont, almost at West Glover (see map).

Above: the **T.O.T.** tree, monitoring instrument box and control console.

Below: two of the accompanying concept notations for the **T.O.T.**

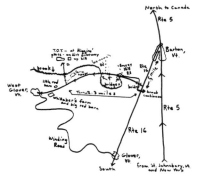

Please make your own reservations for accommodations:

Motels: Aime's Motel (St. Johnsbury), Bayview Motel (Newport), Bear Creek Farms Lodge (Westfield), Border Motel (Derby), Crystal Lake Lodge (Barton), Darion Inn (Lyndonville), Holiday Motel (St. Johnsbury), Inglenook Lodge (North Troy), Jay Peak Lodging Association (Jay Peak), Kelley's (Derby Line), Lynburke Motel (Lyndonville), Lyndon Motel (Lyndon), Maple Center Motel (Saint Johnsbury), Pepin's Motel (Newport), Redwood Motel Inn (Lyndon), Riverside Motor Court (Saint Johnsbury), Sonnenhof Inn (Jay), Starr's Village Motel (North Troy), Top o' the Hill Inn (Newport), Village Motel (Hardwick), Yankee Traveler Motel (Saint Johnsbury).

Hotels: Hotel Newport (Newport), Hotel Reba (North Troy), New Avenue Hotel (Saint Johnsbury), Valley House Hotel (Orleans).

For further information, call 802 / 525-6211.

Vostell's T.O.T.

by Dick Higgins

Newhall, California is a wiggly wagging tongue of the Mohave Desert sticking into the huge suburban slum called Los Angeles. My ambition drafted me and stationed me there, teaching at a madcap mausoleum sponsored by the Disneys, the California Institute of the Arts. In desperation I wrote to Vostell from Newhall, asking him — the most urban and engagé of artists—to do a piece using nature, and specifically offering him the use of one of the rather handsome live oaks on my land. So the **T.O.T.** began to come about, in the winter of 1970, a **T**echnological **O**ak **T**ree.

Of course my relationship with Vostell goes back a lot farther than 1970. Nearly ten years ago we were active together in the founding of the Fluxus movement, and after that in the Yam Festival, various happenings, etc. We collaborated together on a turn-on book for architecture, **Fantastic Architecture,** a collection of fantastic ideas about space and building and physical environment by artists of all kinds, which was done in Germany by Droste Verlag, and in the USA by **Something Else Press,** with which I work, and which also published Vostell's **De-coll/age Happenings,** a collection of Vostell's scenarios up through 1966. Over the years we'd laughed together about how artificial most technological art seemed, as if its sole reason for being were to use as many grants and expensive equipment as possible. We were more impressed by the artists' fund-raising abilty than by any of the individual works.

They seemed thin.

So Vostell dreamed, when I wrote him, and planned, and came up with the concept of a monitoring tree. But when we came to estimate its cost, we were staggered. And in any case, just after that, I became a refugee from Charles Manson-ville.

I ran as far as possible, to Vermont — gentle, quiet but lacking oaks for the most part. In the meantime Vostell was still dreaming of the **T.O.T.**, and working over the project with Peter Saage, a brilliant engineer who has worked with Vostell frequently in recent years, the project became feasible again. Vostell wrote me an exhilerated letter, I said marvelous, and so in the early spring of 1972 Vostell and Saage came to Vermont and the work began—in a maple tree, for which Vermont is famous because of the syrup made from the sap of the tree.

The meaning is different here from in Newhall. There it was an imposition, technologically, of nature onto the hideous and nervous plastic that defines the local life style. Here it is a monitoring tool, an information poem, controlling nothing but proposing a great deal. One takes note of it among other natural phenomena. And the particular maple, in front of my farmhouse, can provide data to be sent all over the world, not only for Vostell's own particular work, but for other artists' conceptions as well.

Barton, Vermont
June 14th, 1972

T.O.T. (Technological Oak Tree)
An environment: consciousness = art

Inauguration: August 19, 1972, 12:00 A.M. to 11:59 P.M.
Place: Old Cisco Farm, West Glover, Vermont (U.S.A.)
Project and Designing Engineer: Peter Saage, Ph.D.
Sponsor: Something Else Gallery, P.O. Box 26, W. Glover, Vt. 05875
Telephone: 802/525-6211

The Idea and Function of the T.O.T.

"T.O.T. is the abbreviation for the 'Technological Oak Tree' because I started my project with an oak tree in the Los Angeles area in 1969. It is n~ w a 20 meter high maple tree in Vermont, on which various physical elements (natural events) **1.** are measured, **2.** are transported to the house, and **3.** are indicated on an idea console, where each measuring instrument is related to an idea file. The user or observer finds for 310 measured readings 310 corresponding ideas: he is free to perform each one after another. Human behavior is triggered by the physical behavior of nature." Wolf Vostell

T.O.T. Idea Console

a) The **evaluation** of the physical elements happens by the translation of physical conditions into direct current readings:

1. 21 **wind** velocities (21 ideas)
2. 90 **temperatures** (90 ideas)
3. 5 **sound** groups (5 ideas)
4. 41 **barometric pressure** readings (41 ideas)
5. 11 **humidity** readings (11 ideas)
6. 41 **light** changes (41 ideas)
7. 100 **time** readings (100 ideas)
8. Indications of **tappable sap** in tree (1 idea)

b) The electronic sensor readings in the tree are transmitted by cable to the console. These values are shown on meters.

c) The T.O.T. console measures approximately 120 x 100 x 160 cm. Under the instrument panel, which holds the meters, is the idea file with 310 cards. To its left and right are identical card files, the one filled with water and the other with earth, to which the tree relates. Interactions between the 310 ideas are possible, so there are 11,520,-000,000,000 (eleven trillion, five hundred twenty billion) potential combinations. The 310 ideas are divided into **thought** events, **visual** events, **touch** events, **driving** events, **smell** events, **telephone** events, **noticing** events, **gift** events, **destruction** events and **construction** events.

Examples

1. Destruction event (temperature +25° F)
Destroy the biggest piece of glass in the house. Have the glazier come and measure the pieces. Set a price and date. Have the glass reinstalled.

2. Touch event (temperature +26° F)
Hold your hands 10 cm above the running water of a stream for one hour: afterwards, go back to the house as slowly as possible.

3. Noticing event (temperature +27° F)
On the idea cards is a photo of a familiar landscape.
Try to photograph the picture in the same landscape.
Expose the film so that no image will register.
Attach the developed blank film to the idea card.

4. Travel event (temperature +28° F)
Climb into your car. Buy forty loaves of bread. Drive forty miles to the south. Give away the forty loaves after those forty miles. Go back home again.

5. Construction event (temperature +29°F, time 1:00 P.M.)
Wrap barbed wire around the T.O.T.

16

Found out by chance

tochis, tuchis, t.o.t. (abbreviation): Yiddish

The "CH" is a gutteral, as in the composer "Bach." You can say it to rhyme with "duck hiss" or with "caucus." It means "beneath" or "under." For instance, a "potch in tochis" is a swat down yonder, and a good threat for children.

"Tochis afn tish" doesn't mean "fanny on the table," its literal meaning. It means, more, "put your cards on the table, put up or shut up." A bit rude.

So one says, "Now let's talk seriously. **T.O.T.** please."

SOMETHING ELSE PRESS, INC.
P. O. BOX 26
WEST GLOVER, VERMONT 05875

Identical Lunch (bottled series)

score: a tunafish sandwich on wheat toast with lettuce and
       butter no mayo, and a glass of buttermilk or a cup
       of soup.
Each of the edition of twenty-three bottled lunches contains
the above score, plus one other ingredient:
1 white wine
2. artesian well water
3. motor oil
4. gasoline
5. buttons
6. fibreglass
7. commercial strawberry frosting
8. human hair
9. broiled for fifteen minutes at 450 degrees
10. candlewax
11. lysol
12. letters and photos
13. cranberry juice
14. baby tomatoes, white, green and red   .
15. sweepings from studio floor
16. one dirty sock
17. rubber glove
18. Waring blended(courtesy George Maciunas)
19. lint from clothes dryer
20. Ajax, Bold detergent, Axion pre-soak and comet cleanser
21. dirt, stones and hay
22. stove bolts
23. nine fresh eggs

Each of the above objects was prepared during the first week of
October of '72 and sealed one month later, with the exception of #4 and
#23. The 23rd bottled lunchs These two are bottled fresh at each viewing.

Alison Knowles

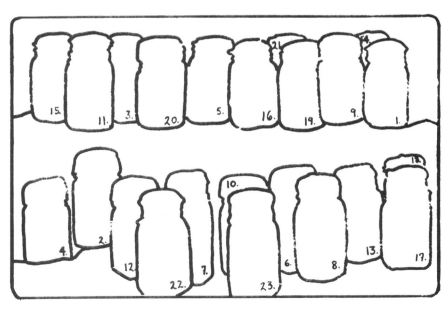

18

19

TOWING A DRAG IN AN UNDERWATER SEARCH

William Burroughs rapping on revolutionary techniques.
Interviewer: Dan Georgakas
London, Summer, 1970

22

DG: Your work is a devastating critique of modern society, but you have not written much about how to deal with the nightmare you describe.

WB: I have done that in my new book, The Job and I will go much further. I've written an actual treatise on revolutionary tactics and weapons. That is a treatise on the actual methods and various revolutionary techniques. A great deal of revolutionary tactics I see now are really 19th century tactics. People think in terms of small arms and barricades, in terms of bombing police stations and post offices like the IRA of 1916. What I'm talking about in The Job and in this treatise, (The Electronic Revolution) is bringing the revolution into the 20th century which includes, above all, the use of mass media. That's where the real battle will be fought.

DG: What about a situation like that in Greece where you have a complete physical oppression, including systematic torture. How do you use media technique there?

WB: You don't. It's too late. You have to use other methods there. America is different. There's an extremely chaotic situation which the revolutionaries can take full advantage of. For instance, there's a growing gap between the mass media and the administration. We're beginning to get an overlap between some liberal elements in the mass media and the underground press. I think this is a very important development. It should be encouraged.

DG: Groups like the Black Panthers have had a certain access to the media. This hasn't prevented them from having their positions distorted and their leadership physically oppressed.

WB: Very different. Very different indeed. I have suggested a number of electronic techniques that might be useful. I suggested the use of cutups in an article published in the Los Angeles Free Press.

DG: Wouldn't something definite like taking out the lights be more practical?

WB: Many of those centers will be guarded very carefully now. Until quite recently, important power structures were quite vulnerable. Rather small detonator charges would have been effective. Let's say something like that was done, it would make chaos, but it wouldn't lead anywhere. But if you could take over the mass media, you could take over the country.

DG: The Establishment knows that very well.

WB: Of course they know it. The players in every game usually know what moves are open to the other players. That doesn't mean they always know the right countermove. Like in war, this side knows what that side is doing, but they don't always have an effective counter.

DG: Historically, the process seems to work out the opposite way. The mass media is able to contain the radical thrust by incorporating it into its complexity like an amiable amoeba.

WB: That's true. It's a very old tactic. The English are particularly goo at that, at absorbing dissident elements. The authorities always try to put dissent into a category where they deal with it more easily. They call the dissenter a bohemian or a radical, a this or a that. It's always a difficult manuever to get something into the mass media. That doesn't mean that it can't be done or isn't being done all the time. The underground press has been very successful, but there's very little use made of ham radio. Ham television is another possibility.

DG: Do you think the Conspiracy 8 made effective use of media?

WB: I don't know quite what to think of that. There's going to be a play here in London based on the trial testimony and I'm going to play Judge Hoffmann. Obviously the defense's objective was to put the whole system on trial in a court of law. They got an awful lot of publicity. They all got sentences, but now they are

going around speaking everywhere. I feel pretty certain they
made their point.

DG: Abbie Hoffmann did something on television that was interesting. He
wore an American flag shirt during one of the late night talk shows.
●●●●●●●●●●●●●●●●●●●●●. Every time he was to speak or when the
camera panned to different guests, there was a blank because such a
shirt can't be broadcast on the airwaves. The discussion was on
civil liberties and censorship. The blank was the best argument
Hoffmann had going. Is that the kind of thing you advocate?

WB: That was very good, but I have very precise techniques in mind,
directions that are really too complicated to give here. I've dealt
with them in <u>The Job</u> and in the treatise mentioned earlier. I think
certain areas have hardly been tapped. Take the festivals. They're
extremely explosive. What could be done with taperecorders is
unlimited. You could cause a riot easily. All you have to do is
take the taperecorders with riot material already recorded and then
record any sort of scuffle that goes on. When you start playing it
back, you're going to have more scuffles. It's very simple, this
staging of events with taperecorders. The CIA and other agencies
have been doing it for years. The CIA was in Paris recording in
the streets ten years ago. It's as simple as this: a recorded
whistle will bring cops, a recorded gunshot when they have their
guns out . . . well . . . it's as simple as that.

DG: You seem to be minimizing the kind of activities a lot of other
people get enthusiastic about, like the new life styles.

WB: The way of dressing is a demonstration and it is useful as such
The whole hippy way of dressing has gone around the world. It
has become an international phenomenon. But once an underground
really goes underground, it can't have a style of dress as such,
it can't have any uniform that announces itself. How long could
the underground against the Nazis have lasted if they all wore
the same clothes and hair styles? How long could the present
underground in the Soviet Union last?

DG: There's been a tremendous resurgence of the use of heroin in the youth culture. It's a flood, often cheaper and easier to get than grass.

WB: Heroin is a drug that is much more to the advantage of the Establishment than grass. I don't want to exaggerate the matter, but it does incapacitate people so they are solely concerned with heroin. This is certainly dangerous from a revolutionary point of view. It's certainly an unprecidented phenomenon. When I was in high school, the idea of a high school student using anything but alchhol was absolutely out of the world. They knew there were people called"dope fiends" but it was quite out of their whole reality. That, of course, began to change in the early sixties. When I was in the states around 1945 there were really no young junkies. They were all middle age or older. Heroin is certainly a pain killer. With so many people, especially in the ghettoj living pratically intolerable lives, it's quite understandable how they could turn to heroin. They tend to take anything that alleviates the condition under which they live. The middle class has other conditions that may be just as bad from another point of view. They suffer from an overall spiritual improvishment. That may be quite as painful as the physical hardships and conditions in the ghetto.

DG: Rather than a counter-attack by the Establishment, the flood of heroin may mean a further breakdown of the system.

WB: Heroin addicts, of course, are not going to be very dangerous to the Establishment. They could be if their supply was insured. The Turkish army used to run on opium. They got quite large amounts of opium, dates, and sugar in their rations. Addicts are capable of doing very strenuous work and they are not as subject to fatigue as the non-addicted. Some of the hardest work in the Far East is done by addicts, especially in rural India. That is a case of people who are leading extremely rigorous lives. They work hard all the time. Addicts can function. What is so incapacitating about heroin in terms of the modern Establishment is its high price and the fact that addicts have to steal in order to get the money. Keeping up their habit takes up practically all their time. It's not so much that they are physically incapacitated. Even here in England, it's becoming increasingly like America. They're closing down clinic after clinic. Very few doctors here want to prescribe for addicts.

*G: You spoke of the underground press before. You are one of the few figures who has access to almost any of the large circulation magazines yet who still choses to publish much of his work in the underground newspapers and mimeographed literary magazines. Why is that?

WB: I think the underground presses are very useful. They reach a very special audience and those people are very definitely my readers. I've written a good deal about the underground press as the only counter to the mass media, which is, as I said before, now beginning to overlap with the underground in some areas.

G: Do you think wallposters are effective counter-media weapons?

WB: We got an awful lot of that in France and China. I don't know just how effective it is to scratch up a slogan or put up a poster. I think it has some kind of immediate impact, but it wears off quickly. You could try writing slogans on widows with flouride. Then they have to remove the whole plate or leave the slogan up. It's a good angle. You do that to a huge department store window and they have a dilemma. You've actually made a revolutionary etching.

DG: Have you studied the use of media in the Chinese Cultural Revolution The cult of personality is distressing, but it seems Mao is letting his young people carry on a serious struggle against his own bureaucrats and authoritarians.

WB: I think that is precisely what he is doing. I think he is
concerned that the Chinese Revolution does not go the way of the
Russian Revolution with a new elite of bureaucrats and managers,
a privileged class society. I think the Cultural Revolution is
terribly interesting. Communist China is the only country in the
world that has the support of its young people. I think that's the
real reason for the travel ban the State Department has put on
China. They're afraid to have people go there and realize that
this is not a fake, that any Establishment that offers its young
people something meaningful and valuable will get their
support. (The travel ban on Americans to China has recently been
lifted but there seems little likelihood that any large number
of Americans will be traveling to China in the near future).

DG: Films seem to be an increasingly important medium in the youth
culture.

WB: They are extremely important. I mean the impact of a film like
Easy Rider is terrific.

DG: Europeans seem to make much more of that particular film than
Americans do.

WB: I think that's because of the time lag. England is always about
ten years behind. They will be closer and closer to America in
the future. They saw the American exotica in Easy Rider, that
thing that was made Damon Runyon so popular, this strange
exotic land called America. I think a film like The Damned is
even more instructive. Most young people don't realize to what
extent everything that goes on is controlled by a very few
people. That film showed how one word from one man and one woman
controlled the whole Reich's arsenal and police power. They had
to get the okay of the Krupp family before they could get rid of
the S.A. The same is true in every industrialized country. The

The real power is invested in the hands of the big industrial
families. In Germany, it was in the hands of the Krupps. Of
course, in America you have many more families, but I think the
same is true. That's where the real orders come from, not from
Nixon or any of those front people. I think revolutionaries
overemphasize the importance of people like Nixon.

DG: That sounds like an orthodox Marxist analysis.

WB: I don't know if it's Marxist or not. It's just the facts. They
have the power. They are the ones for whom the Establishment is
advantageous. There's no mystery about that. A very small
number of people control all the money, privileges, positions of
wealth. A very very few people benefit and they intend to keep it
that way. They'll go to any lengths to keep it. Marx was writing
about people, and he was extending it into the future. He was a
prophet. I think it's a clear case of someone getting himself up
as a prophet. Lenin did the same thing, but he was also a political
leader.

DG: Marx also involved himself in practical political work. The
popular image is of the old graybeard locked up in the British
Museum, but he was very involved in day to do problems.

WB: I don't know much about that. A person can be both. Trotsky was
very definitely both.

DG: Have you ever done cut-ups of political material?

WB: I have, yes. It can be done with considerable effectiveness. It
could be quite possible to cut up someone's speech and shoot it
right back at him. It's more advantageous to get out such a cut-up
speech on ham radio while the original speech is still on. I know of
a case where a political speech and a number of political writings
were fed into a computer. They came out in complete syntax, perfect
sentences. It sounded extremely credible and plausible, but it was

completely meaningless. There are a number of tricks like
that. You can take a speech and cut in sneezes and coughs
and pig grunts, anything you want, and get it right out while
he's still speaking. Another thing you can do is stop someone
from talking by using a tape recorder. You play back what he
is saying ten seconds after he has said it. Within a very
short time, he can't talk. Try it sometime. I've seen people
who can repeat what you're saying right after you say it. You
just can't go on talking.

DG: Such strategems seem to get us farther and farther from art. The
avant-garde likes to shout about the death of art rom time to
time, but we seem to be experiencing it.

WB: I'm talking about weapons, not works of art. Literary use of
cut-ups and tapes is quite another matter. It's a question of
survival. I don't want to live under a junta ●●●●●●●●●●●●●●● of
●●●●●# colonels, especially A-erican colonels. I woul-n't live very
long. They would have to go much farther in America than in
smaller countries because you have possibly forty million
opponents to the regime. Now, what do they propose to do with all
those people? I would venture ,o guess they would have to
institute extermination programs. You coul'n't put that many
people in concentration camps. You wouldn't have enough people
to guard them. It would require a tremendous network to feed and
supply such camps. This isn't like the Japanese-Americans in
World War II. We're talking about tens of millions.

DG: How could an Establishment capable of that allow its media to be
used against it in any significant manner?

WB: They are not always able to prevent things like that. Power is
not unlimited. They must have pretexts. They must have an excuse
to proceed. They couldn't start things like that without a
pretext of war or some extreme emergency.

DG: Such a pretext could be manufactured.

WB: Yes, they could put an old style a-bomb over New York which would
eliminate quite a bit of the trouble, and then say the Chinese did
it.

DG: They don't need anything so drastic. They can use the scapegoat of
the blacks just as the Germans used the Jews.

WB: I think they have to go further than that. They have to scare
everyone in America. Too many people would see through using the
Negroes.

DG: Many activists feel media politics are extremely limited. They
feel they have to physically attack even if they only produce more
chaos. They reason that even that would help the various
liberation movements around the world.

WB: Well, America is certainly vulnerable. America is extremely
vulnerable to chaos, to a breakdown in communications, particularly
to a breakdown in the food supply. Bombs concentrated on just
communications random bombs on trains, boats, planes, buses could
lead to paralysis. But you must consider the available counters. We
spoke about the ultimate repression that would be used. Once
largescale bombing started you could expect the most violent
reaction. They'd declare a national emergency and arrest anyone.
They don't have to know who did it. They'll just arrest everyone
who might have done it.

DG: American writers tend to have a distaste for politics, but like
many of them, you seem to be dealing increasingly with political
problems.

WB: Any writer, especially any American writer, cannot be indifferent
to political questions because it is a matter of his own survival.
They're going to be the first to get the axe if Wallace and his ilk
ever get power because they've said so quite frankly. They realize
the importance of the writer. I think it's a matter of survival.
Any writer must line up with the liberal left unless he wants a
place with the right.

DB: Is there some kind@ of middle ground, that objective plane the universities like to project?

WB: No.

DG: You've made wide use of the phrase "Nothing is true, everything is permitted." What does that mean?

WB: Those are the last wor s of Hassan i Sabbah, the old man of the mountain. It means that if everything is an illusion, then everything is permitted. When things become real, efinite, then they are not permitted. Now, our culture, by and large, absolutely revers that——everything is true and not ing is permitted. That is the whole stand of the reactionary Establishment: Make everything true and permit nothing.

                              ---William Burroughs
                              Dan Georgakas
                              London, August, 1970

Georgakas
Box 327
Glen Gardner, NJ
08826

34-24 32ND S←
    ASTOP IA
GUEENS, NYC
        11106

274-4413

L'éternité

JEAN-FRANÇOIS BORY

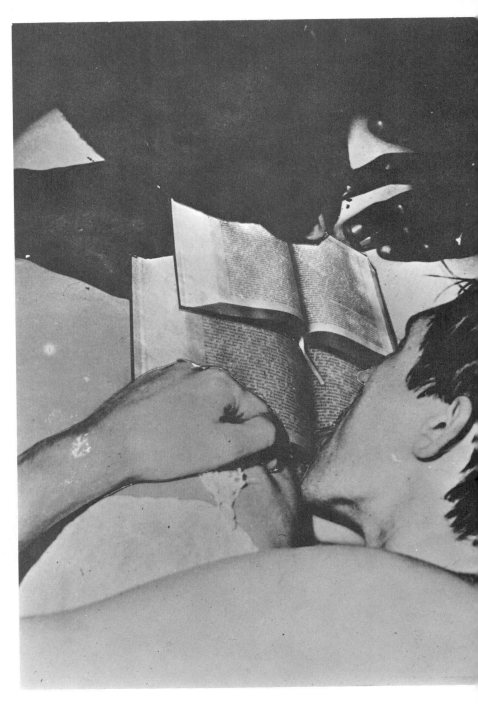

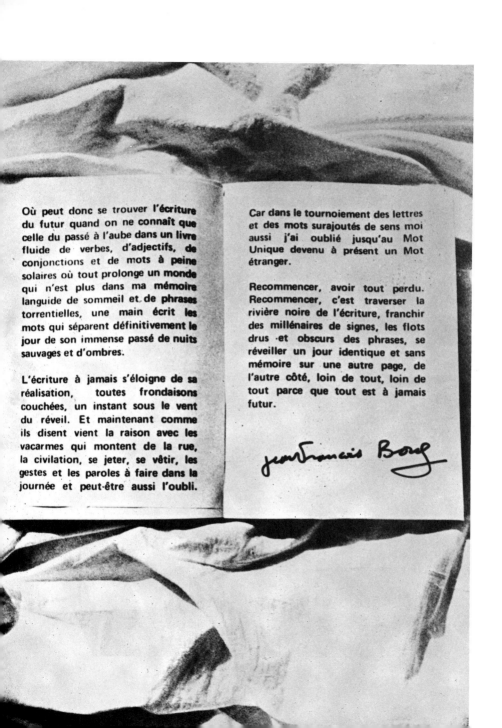

Où peut donc se trouver l'écriture du futur quand on ne connaît que celle du passé à l'aube dans un livre fluide de verbes, d'adjectifs, de conjonctions et de mots à peine solaires où tout prolonge un monde qui n'est plus dans ma mémoire languide de sommeil et de phrases torrentielles, une main écrit les mots qui séparent définitivement le jour de son immense passé de nuits sauvages et d'ombres.

L'écriture à jamais s'éloigne de sa réalisation, toutes frondaisons couchées, un instant sous le vent du réveil. Et maintenant comme ils disent vient la raison avec les vacarmes qui montent de la rue, la civilation, se jeter, se vêtir, les gestes et les paroles à faire dans la journée et peut-être aussi l'oubli.

Car dans le tournoiement des lettres et des mots surajoutés de sens moi aussi j'ai oublié jusqu'au Mot Unique devenu à présent un Mot étranger.

Recommencer, avoir tout perdu. Recommencer, c'est traverser la rivière noire de l'écriture, franchir des millénaires de signes, les flots drus et obscurs des phrases, se réveiller un jour identique et sans mémoire sur une autre page, de l'autre côté, loin de tout, loin de tout parce que tout est à jamais futur.

Jean-François Borg

I am sitting in a room (1970)

Necessary equipment:

    1 microphone
    2 tape recorders
    amplifier
    1 loudspeaker

Choose a room the musical qualities of which you would like to evoke.

Attach the microphone to the input of tape recorder #1.

To the output of tape recorder #2 attach the amplifier and loudspeaker.

Use the following text or any other text of any length:

> "I am sitting in a room different from the one you are in now.
> I am recording the sound of my speaking voice and I am going to play it back into the room again and again until the resonant frequencies of the room reinforce themselves so that any semblance of my speech, with perhaps the exception of rhythm, is destroyed.
> What you will hear, then, are the natural resonant frequencies of the room articulated by speech.
> I regard this activity not so much as a demonstration of a physical fact, but more as a way to smooth out any irregularities my speech might have."

Record your voice on tape through the microphone attached to tape recorder #1.

Rewind the tape to its beginning, transfer it to tape recorder #2, play it back into the room through the loudspeaker and record a second generation of the original recorded statement through the microphone attached to tape recorder #1.

Rewind the second generation to its beginning and splice it onto the end of the original recorded statement on tape recorder #2.

Play the second generation only back into the room through the loudspeaker and record a third generation of the original recorded statement through the microphone attached to tape recorder #1.

Continue this process through many generations.

All the generations spliced together in chronological order make a tape composition the length of which is determined by the length of the original statement and the number of generations recorded.

Make versions in which one recorded statement is recycled through many rooms.

Make versions using one or more speakers of different languages in different rooms.

Make versions in which, for each generation, the microphone is moved to different parts of the room or rooms.

Make versions that can be performed in real time.

Alvin Lucier
March 1970
Middletown, Connecticut

D.S.: What's your attitude toward playing tape in a performance...making a performance out of playing tape?

A.L.: I was always against that. Well, I wasn't <u>always</u> against it. All of us who made pieces with electronics started with tape because tape enables you to play with sounds in a particular way that I don't think any other medium enables you to do. We all started in tape studios because that's where electronics was going on. But you soon get very tired of that because people are more interesting than tapes. Outside is more interesting than inside, if you know what I mean. I would prefer to spend a day outside in environments with people, or in auditoriums, or in schools, than to spend it cooped up in some small studio space. And being an old performer, I feel that live performances are more interesting than dead performances. Tape enables us to discover things about sound that we had hitherto been unable to discover. But that prepared us to go on and do more interesting things in the live performing situation. It isn't as safe a situation as making the tape because in a live performance electronic devices break down and things don't work. But we always keep tape as a way to store sounds which we could bring into a live performance.
      with
Now,/this piece we're talking about, <u>I am sitting in a room</u>, I didn't choose to use tape. I had to. I was forced to in order to recycle the sounds back into the space again and again. The only way was to have tapes. That tape wasn't just a place to compose sounds, that tape was a tool---the conveyor of the sound so that I could send it back into the space again and again. Without tape I wouldn't have been able to do this version of the piece.

D.S.: In other words, the piece never reaches performance until all the generations of the original statement and what follows are played back all together.

A.L.: Right.

D.S.: When you worked on materials for the piece, there was never a moment until all those generations had been spliced together that the piece was complete? Is it only complete in performance...when you play the whole thing?

A.L.: Yes. That's funny because if I had consulted an engineer about this he would

probably have found a way that I could have got the end result in one process, one fast
process, or one generation. There are ways to ~~talk to a tape machine,~~ by-pass ~~the~~
~~tain~~ erase heads, ~~on things like that.~~ Or ~~by making a particular~~ loops, big loop S
which could get the end result very fast. But what I was interested in was the process ,
the step-by-step, slow process of the disintegration of the speech and the reinforcement of the resonant frequencies. We went over to Polaroid because (~~my wife,~~ Mary) as you
know, did a visual analogue to this with a Polaroid snapshot which she (then) subjected
to a reproductive situation where she would reproduce the original, reproduce the reproduction of that, and so on. The director of the art department at Polaroid said,
when he saw the end results: "Well, I could do that in one step." He just didn't understand what we thought was particularly interesting about this process. We were interested in the gradual process itself and that takes a long time. It takes a (~~sort of~~) mechanical process to bring about.

D.S.: You've also discarded one of the values of accurate tape recording...namely that
by reproducing the thing so many times all the parameters that manufacturers strive to
achieve in their tape recorder, like accuracy and fine frequency response, are destroyed
by playing back in the room. You're not using the machine in exactly the way it could
best be used according to the manufacturer.

A.L.: Well, I don't agree with that. People sometimes don't understand the process that
I've employed. They think that I re-record the same paragraph or speech from one tape
machine to another, and each time a recording is made the quality of the copy degene-
rates a little bit. But it's not that at all. It's playing the speech back into the
space, in other words, the signal goes through the air again. It's not reproduced
electronically. It's reproduced acoustically. (~~So that We did~~ use Nagras, very excellent tape
machines. And, on this particular version I made fifteen generations of the same
speech and you don't hear must distortion or disintegration of the tape matter. In
fact, the machines did a very good job of maintaining it. It's the space that destroys
the speech. The air destroys the speech.

D.S.: What I meant to say was that an engineer would probably say you've done a really
~~pretty damn fine~~ reproducing the thing, when, of course, what you had in mind was to get out

poor job of reproducing the thing when, of course, what you had in mind was to get out
of the machines, to get the material into a new area on its way to being regenerated.

A.L.:   Yes.

D.S.:   How did you get the idea in the first place?

A.L.:   I got the idea from a friend of mine, Edmund Dewan, ~~who was~~ a physicist who collaborated with me on my brainwave piece in 1965. He had gone to a talk on speakers given,
I think, by ~~a man named~~ Bose who designed a particular loudspeaker which takes into
account situations exactly like the one I'm trying to work in. He heard examples of
instruments being played in the space again and again, and what happened to them. And
he told me that it might be interesting if I experimented along these particular lines,
which I did. I tried to find the most direct, simple way of bringing this about.
When I say that, I mean I didn't try to program a wide variety of speech sounds, for
(someone specific in mind?)
example, like another composer might do, inventing a lot of interesting sounds which,
if you recycled them, would show that the space acts as a filter, filtering out all
of the frequencies except the resonant frequencies.

D.S.:   And it reinforces those.

A.L.:   Yes. Now I considered composing a wide variety of sounds to put into the space,
to get a very interesting wide variety of resonant frequencies or to see what would
come from that. But I tossed that idea out because it was so similar to other ideas
that composers have when they make pieces on tape with speech. Since I've been acting
in those Dr. Chicago films I have started paying attention to my particular speech,
the things which are original to my speech and don't sound like anybody else's. I
thought I could use the electronic situation along with this phenomenon of resonant
frequencies in a room to iron out or to smooth out the complex speech sounds that I
get because I do have a speech impediment---you know I'm a stutterer---instead of
trying to invent interesting speech sounds. I discovered that I have interesting
speech sounds anyway, and I don't have to invent them because I already have. A person who stutters or has a lisp invents that from the beginning. I didn't need to
invent it artificially. And I always like to make the situation as personal as I
possibly can when I deal with electronics. In my brainwave piece I really wasn't

interested in what the frequency of the brainwaves were, what the formant structure was
or anything like that. I was interested in the performance of one man, sitting alone,
producing sounds without having to move by employing high-gain amplifiers to bring this
very personal thing about. Of course, everyone in the audience is in touch with that
because they have brainwaves too. Now in the speech piece, while everybody does not
stutter, I think everyone has a certain amount of anxiety about speech. I've met a
lot of people who I don't think stutter but they think they do. Bob Ashley, for instance, thinks he stutters...I wouldn't have thought that he did, but if he thinks he
does that's an interesting situation. If he thinks he does, then perhaps a lot of people
think they do. In that case, I would feel that I'm in touch with people on that particular plane. For example, if you write a song and you talk about death, birth, or
romance, you touch people because they think about that all the time. And in most
electronic compositions that I hear, I often feel that composers are out of touch with
that personal contact. I want to use electronics simply as a particular means to touch
                                                                     particularly
people in the audience. I don't care/much about circuitry or things of that kind but
I do care about what electronics can do for me to help me touch people. That's why I
want to write a piece for the phone because people call on the phone all the time.
They have terrific anxiety about calling and answering the phone. On the other hand,
they find the phone very very valuable. I'm not interested in these resonant frequencies of spaces in a scientific way as much as I am in opening a secret door to the
sound situation that you experience when you're in a particular room. I want to evoke
the ideas of a particular room. If you sit in a room, and you talk in a room to friends,
and you drink in a room, and play recordings in a room, the size and shape of the room
has a tremendous amount to do with how you hear the sounds. I feel as though I'm in
the same situation as composers felt they were in when they first started perceiving
overtones. (I mean, overtones are always in pitch. If you strike a pitch there are always a whole series of overtones.) Musicians were always aware of them, I think, but
they weren't defined until someone really discovered that overtones were, in fact, a
physical phenomenon. And then the whole question of western polyphony was explained
by the fact that the simple triads are replicas of the most simple overtones as they
occur---the octave, the fifth, the fourth, the third, and on up. I feel almost as if

[margin handwritten notes:] Should explain of overtones & can do without.

we're in the same situation but we're just beginning to perceive that ~~a pitch is~~ very definable and observable. It's because ~~we~~ have these electronic devices that enable us to discover this thing overtly. I'm very pleased to be in on these first experiments. But, I'm particularly interested in evoking the reminiscence of a particular room.that I've been in. I did a version of I am sitting in a room in the Brandeis electronic studio, (~~which is~~ a very small room filled with electronic equipment)which I didn't ever feel very pleased to be in. The resonant frequencies got reinforced after the fifth or sixth generation because the room was very bright, one/wall was a ~~immediately~~ plate glass window. The version that I just did here in my apartment I enjoy a lot because it took longer time to achieve the resonant frequencies...due, I think, to the wall-to-wall carpeting, which is very strange because when we came into this apartment we didn't think we wanted this wall-to-wall carpeting. But we've learned two things: one is that if you have ̢it people enjoy sitting on the floor which they wouldn't feel like doing in a place like the Brandeis electronic studio; and two, the carpeting and the drapes on the wall, which we didn't enjoy much either, cut down the production of the resonant frequencies, and it took a longer time to achieve them. But it gave us a more interesting result. So you see how doing processes like this can change your mind about things.

D.S.:   It's interesting that the personality of the room is what irons out the peculiarities of your speech.

A.L.:   Right.

D.S.:   You thought about that beforehand?

A.L.:   Yes. I thought about it. What I'm doing at the present time is experimenting in other spaces. For instance, I'm not quite sure but didn't we get a different set of pitch intervals in the Brandeis studio than we did here in this room? Do you remember what they were?

D.S.:   It seems to me that we got two sets of fifths in both of them. But they were much more complex in this version.

A.L.:   Did you notice that tunes seemed to come in? What interests me also is that, while the speech gets destroyed, you don't ever destroy the rhythmic aspect which you can always hear. I'm just dying to try it with other people speaking different languages

where the speed and the articulation and the accentual qualities change. What I would
want to do some time is to send a set of instructions to friends of mine in other parts
of the world, in Stockholm or in Japan, and so forth, and have them do the same thing.
Also, what I would like to do is to carry the process further and further. (my wife)
did the visual version, she took a picture of the same chair that I sat in when I made
the tape here, and she subjected it to the Polaroid process fifty-two times. It was
very interesting because we put a slight error into the reproduction process so that
every time she made a copy it made the image slightly enlarged---but of course the picture stayed the same size so the image began to move off the picture. There was a dark
shadow behind the lamp which stayed in the photo and which stayed on the reproductions
and finally/the fifty-second reproduction it was simply black. The shadow behind the
lamp grew until it took up the whole image. Of course a lot of dirt started to get on
the reproductions, so that at the end it looks like a star map. Indeed, a friend of
mine who was at one of the performances came up and said towards the end that it looked
just like Job's Coffin, which is apparently a part of the stars.

D.S.: Is it an extension of the idea of personal relevance that you chose that particular
text to use?

A.L.: I wanted to choose a text that wouldn't be "arty". One of your first impulses is
to find an interesting text---Joyce, for instance. But I didn't want to. It's like the
bat piece, Vespers, I didn't want the input to have much of interest about it semantical-
ly. I wanted the interest to come in the speech peculiarities which I have. And, of
course, I want other people to do it too because everyone has interesting speech.
There isn't anyone you meet who doesn't. Secondly, I wanted the process to do the work.
The room space finishes the job. So, what I did was explain that to the people in the
audience. The explanation was really built into the piece. But you'd be surprised how
many people come up afterwards and don't know what I've done. The paragraphs were
repeated fifteen times, twelve of which are pretty comprehensible---and still people
come up to me and say "How did you do this? Did you use electronic distorting devices?"
And so forth.

D.S.:   Do you consider that statement a score of the piece?

A.L.:   I'd kind of like it to be, but I don't think it's complete enough. I think it's
a score only to people who have done some work in this kind of thing. If I sent this
piece to a composer who worked in electronics I think he would understand. But it's
not publishable.for a general audience. I have to think up a way to make it so.

D.S.:   Do you think a score of an electronic piece is a different animal from a score
of conventional notation?

A.L.:   I don't know. The only reason I would want to make a score is so that other people
could perform the process.in spaces of their own.

D.S.:   So you'd include information as to how you used two tape recorders?

A.L.:   Right.

D.S.:   I guess what I'm interested in is how far your idea about the piece extends into
the mechanics of achieving it. In other words, if someone else uses one of the other
things you mentioned, like a loop, do you think that's doing this piece o r is it new?

A.L.:   Well, I think the piece is subject to a lot of versions. Actually, I'm supposed to
do this in Japan at the Pepsi Pavilion (which is a big pavilion). It's got a big dome
and it has a lot of tape machines and speakers and microphones. So I'm going to try
to figure out a way to do the piece in a totally live performance where I would have
people talking and a continuous replaying of tapes and recycling of the speech into
the Pepsi pavilion. This would constitute a live performance. I've by no means decided
fully on how it should be done. Also, I must admit, I enjoyed making a tape. Mary
made a set of fifty-two slides so that we have a portable piece that's very easy to
perform, twenty-two minutes long, tape and slides. And I rather enjoy that because
now most composers are going against tape. They're jumping on the live performance
bandwagon and I enjoyed going back and making a tape piece.

Sonic Meditations
Dedicated to the Ǫ ensemble and Amelia Earhart

Pauline Oliveros
March - November 1971

Sonic Meditations are intended for group work over a long period
of time with regular meetings. No special skills are necessary. Any
persons who are willing to commit themselves can participate. The Ǫ
ensemble to whom these meditations are dedicated has found that non-
verbal meetings intensify the results of these meditations and help
provide an atmosphere which is conducive to such activity. With
continious work some of the following becomes possible with sonic
meditations: Heightened states of awareness or expanded consciousness,
changes in physiology and psychology from known and unknown tensions to
represent the tuning of mind and body. The group develops positive
energy which can influence others who are less experienced. Members of
the group achieve greater awareness and sensitivity to each other.
Music is a welcome by product of this activity.

I

Teach yourself to fly
Any number of persons sit in a circle facing the center. Illuminate
the space with dim blue light. Begin by simply observing your own breathing.
Always be a deserver. Gradually observe your breathing become audible.
Then gradually introduce your voice. Color your breathing very softly at
first with sound. Let the intensity increase very slowly as you observe it.
Continue as long as possible and until all others are quiet.
Variation: Translate voice to an instrument.

II

Search for a natural or artificial canyon, forest or deserted municipal
quad. Perform. Teach yourself to fly in this space.

Pacific Tell

Find your place in a darkened indoord space or a deserted out of doors
area. Mentally form a sound image. Assume that the magnitude of your concentration on this sound image will cause one or more of the grpup to receive
this sound image by telepathic transmission. Visualize the person to whom
you are sending. Rest after your attempted telepathic transmission by
becoming mentally blank. When or if a sound image different from your own
forms in your mind, assume that you are receiving from someone else, then
make that sound image audible. Rest again by becoming mentally blank or
return to your own mental sound image. Continue as long as possible and
until all others are quiet.

IV

Divide into two or more groups. Each group must have a tape recorder
and be sound isolated from the other groups. The distance might be small
or great i.e. thousand of miles or light years.

Each group then performs pacific tell, attempting inter group or
inter stellar telepathic transmission. A specific time period may be pre
arranged. Each group tape records its own sounds during the telepathic
transmission period for later comparison.

Variation: Instead of working in groups each participant works as an
isolated soloist.

V

Native

Take a walk at night. Walk so silently that the bottoms of your feet
become ears.

VI

Sonic Rorschach

With a white or random noise generator, flood a darkened room with
white noise for thirty minutes or much longer. The band width of the white
noise should be as broad as the limits of the audio range. A pre recorded
tape or a mechanical source such as an air compressor may be substituted
for the generator if necessary. All participants should be comfortably
seated or lying down for the duration of the meditation.. Halfway through
introduce one brilliant flash ▒▒▒▒ of light or one loud, short pulse.

The high intensity flash source could be a photo lamp flash or one puls of a strobe light. If a sound pulse is substituted for the light flash, it must necessarily be of higher amplitude than the white noise.

Variations: a) Find a natural source of white noise such as a water fall or the ocean and go there for this meditation.

b) If the white noise generator is flat, equalize until the source is apparently flat for the human ear.

c) Do this meditation with a different band width represented in subsequent meditations such as one octave at 5K to 10hz.

Have you ever heard the sound of an iceberg melting?

Begin this meditation with the greeting meditation (IX). At the designated time for all persons to be present, begin an eight to fifteen minute imperceptible dimming of the house lights down to as dark as possible. When the lights are about halfway down begin the flood of white noise at the threshold of audibility. Slowly make an imperceptible crescendo to a pre-determined sound level, safe for human ears.

Approximately twenty to thirty minutes later introduce one brilliant light flash. After an hour from the beginning has passed, begin projections on the walls of colorful mandalas, patterns resembling the aurora borealis or simply colors of the spectrum. The light intensity of these projections should be no greater than the threshold of visability or just noticible.

These may continue for approximately thirty minutes. Thirty minutes before the white noise ends. The space should be illuminated by white light slowly over about eight minutes from the threshold of visability to as brilliant as possible. The brilliance must exceed normal house lighting and approach the intensity of daylight. The end of the light and sound should be sudden and synchronous. Darkness and silence should be maintained for ten minutes or more, then illuminate the space with dim blue light for continued meditation in silence and finally exit of the participants. The duration of this meditation is approximately two to four hours or more. All adjustments of light and sound intensity should be pre-set and preferably voltage controlled in order that all present may participate in the meditation, and that activities extraneous to meditation may be avoided. Participants must be comfortable, either sitting or lying down.

Variation: If multiple speakers are used for the production of white noise
one or two persons per speaker could perform meditation movements such as
Tai Chi in front of the speakers at a distance of two to four feet thus
creating sound shadows. The sound shadows could gradually be complemented
by visable shadows activated by just noticible light sources. The duration
of this part of the meditation could be approximately thirty to forty
minutes and succeed or overlap the just noticible projected images.

VII

Removing the demon or getting your rocks off.

Sit in a circle with persons facing in and out alternately. If number in
group is odd, seat the left over person in the center. Each person except
the center person has a pair of resonant rocks. Begin the meditation by
establishing mentally a tempo as slow as possible. Each person begins
independently to strike the rocks together full force maintaining the
imaged tempo. When enough energy is present, shout a pre-meditated word,
once selected the word remains the same. The shout is free of the
established tempo, and may occur one or more times during the meditation.
The center person is without rocks and selects a word, phrase or sentence to
say or in tone repeatedly either silently or audibly for the duration of the
meditation.

Variation: a) Persons without rocks may surround the circle and follow the
        same instructions as the center person, independently.

      b) Persons may repeat mentally or actually one body movement as
        slowly as possible. One body movement may be simple or very
        complicated as long as it is continuous and can be repeated
        exactly as a cycle. Kinetic participants could include the
        shout or the repeated word, phrase or sentence.

      c) Do this meditation in an out door environment. Move slowly
        away from the circle. Move anywhere in the environment but
        keep in audible contact with at least one other person. G
        Gradually return to the beginning circle.

VIII

Environmental Dialogue

Each person finds a place to be, either near to or distant from the others,
either in doors or out-of-doors. Begin the meditation by observing your
own breathing. As you become aware of sounds from the environment, gradually

begin to reinforce the pitch of the sound source. Reinforce either vocally, mentally or with an instrument. If you lose touch with the source, wait quietly for another, reinforce means to strengthen or sustain.

Environmental Dialogue for the New Hampshire Festival Orchestra to Mary and Tom Nee.

On-lake Winnepansaukee at sun up or sun down, players of the orchestra are dispersed heterogeneously in small groups in boats all over the lake. Players begin by observing your own breathing. As you become aware of sounds in the environment, gradually begin to reinforce the pitch of the sound source or its resonance. If you become louder than the source, deminuendo until you can hear it again. If the source disappears listen quietly for another. If thesource is intermittant your pitch reinforcement may be continuous until the source stops. Aural awareness of the source is necessary at all times even though your reinforcement may be momentarily louder. Reinforcement is distinctly different than imitation. Only strengthen or sustain pitch. Allow the boats to drift unless guidance past obstacles or away from shore becomes necessary.

The Flaming Indian. For Gerald Shapiro and Margot Blum.

Tape record a selected environment alone or with a group. Place the microphone carefully in one location. Do the environmental dialogue mentally while you are recording. Reinforce everything you hear mentally. When the meditation is complete, make a translation of the environmental dialogue in the following ways: Reinforce the pitches of the recorded sounds with vocal, instrumental, electronic or a combination of these sources. The resulting translation may exist in one or more channels as the translated sounds only or a combination of the translation and original dialogue.

A new dialogue is then performed in the same or a different environment with the recorded translation and a soloist or a group, either vocal, instrumental or electronic or any combination. The live dialogue should include the sounds of the live environment as well as the recorded translation.

IX

The Greeting or before the Meeting

Begin at least a half hour before the meeting by observing your breathing. Gradually from a pitch image mentally. Maintain the same pitch image for

the duration of the meditation. Whenever a person enters the space produce a
your pitch image as a long tone. Remain silently focused on your sare
pitch image until another person enters the space. Continue until everyone
is present.

X

Sit in a circle with your eyes closed. Begin by observing your own
breathing. Gradually form a mental image of one person who is sitting in
the circle. Sing a long tone to that person. Then sing the pitch that
person is singing. Change your mental image to another person and repeat
until you have contacted every person in the circle one or more times.

XI

Bowl Gong

Sit in a circle with a Japanese Bowl Gong in the center. One person
when ready to begin hands the striker to someone else in the circle. That
person strikes the gong. Each person maintains the pitch mentally for as
long as possible. If the image is lost then the person who has lost it
hands the striker to someone else in the circle. This person again activates
the gong in order to renew the mental pitch image. Continue as long as pos
possible.

XII

One Word

Choose a word. Dwell on this word, write it down as slowly as possible.
Visualize the word with eyes closed and with eyes open. Hear it in
different voices. Mix the voices together. Visualize the word in different
kinds of writing and printing in sizes from microscopic to gigantic, two
dimensional and three dimensional. Slowly and gradually begin to voice the
word. Explore each sound in the word extremely slowly continue repeating
the word. Increase the speed of each repetition imperceptibly. When top
speed has been reached, slow down again imperceptibly.

LADISLAV   NEBESKY

TRIANGLES

a play
in three acts
with prologue
and
epilogue

dramatis personae:

---a---   /anthony/

---e---   /evelina/

--- i ---   /ian/

---o---   /olga/

---u---   /urban/

---y---   /yvonne/

prologue

- - - a - - -
- - - e - - -

- - - i - - -
- - - o - - -

- - - u - - -
- - - y - - -

act one

act two

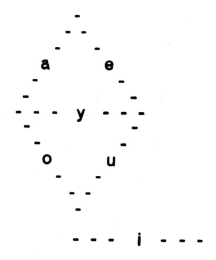

act three

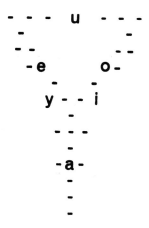

epilogue

```
- - - u - - -
- - - e - - -

- - - i - - -
- - - y - - -

- - - a - - -
- - - o - - -
```

SHIT NO! TEN YEARS AFTER

by Boris Lurie

The art world market in in deep crisis and has been for some
time. Artificial cultivation of decorative 'esthetic' values, reckless
investment speculation aided by large numbers of collaborating artists
have brought about a situation very much like the last stage of a
bull market on the stock exchange. Esthetically and philosophically
the bottom has already dropped out. The mini-movements cultivating
minor esthetic modes by-passed by the pioneers of modern art are being
groomed, refined, enlarged, and overstated all out of proportion to
their real value. Even amputated splinters of the old rebellious Dada
have been converted into saleable parlor games. It is the small
investors deathly frightened of inflation who pursue their favorite
penny-stocks now at overinflated values.

The 'theoretical' part of the art market is supported by museum
curators eager to please trustees and to promote large attendance by
the uneducated public. It is indebted to artist-producers who operate
manufacturing enterprises out of mammoth lofts in New York. But the
sanctity and reliability of art critics and art publications , whose
full page, awe-inspiring ads and color covers have lost their magic,
convince the public no longer. The museums are finally accepted for
what they really are: corporate entities & private organizations
controlled by a small number of not-disinterested trustees whose conflicting interests in the art market should be opened to question.
Such Sanctum Sanctorums have only been picketed, a general clean-up
must begin in earnest. And many artists do understand now that their

field is not just the production of art. In the most extreme cases, political confrontation has become an art form. Some are in flight from marketable objects in what is viewed as an exaggerated reaction to their unhappy findings. To many, unfortunately, all art has become useless and corrupt.

The hope is that some place, some day, a truly unmanipulated art will appear; that younger artists will become free of the art world hang-ups of their older brothers and sisters of the fifties and sixties, and of the poisonous atmosphere of establishment-fostered art. Let's hope they will know better how to handle the success-monster, the ego-monster, the competition-monster, and the monster of in-group camp. These nasty monsters have always had a habit of re-appearing.

The first rebellion always begins out of desperation, triggered perhaps by the realization that isolation and inwardness must be broken. The artist who understands this is free only in rebellion.

My show 'Adieu Amerique' in 1959 was a statement of rejection. I was about to leave New York, and America, for good I thought, and I painted my farewell as it all came pouring out. Paradoxically, this force of rejection and negation turned into an organized activity by a group of artists, Sam Goodman, Stanley Fischer, and I, who established the March Group on 10th Street, later to be nicknamed the 'no-artists'. Our combined mental desperation gave us the courage to cut the cords attaching us to the art world in open, public fashion. We published statements concurrent with our shows that made it impossible to return to the fold, and to cut off such a return should our rebellion have faltered.

We were opposed to the mute chest-beating of the Abstract-Expressionist esthetic, to its refusal to be outspoken and concrete, to its romantic, ivory tower isolation fraught with ambitious power struggles. We were determined to cry out, to say everything at the expense of good table manners, to dispense with an idea of art which prevented action. We felt that the break had to be made absolute. 'Adieu Amerique' brought our personal confessions into the open. It required social and political content. Indeed it brought content back into art openly and without apology, an act copiously avoided at that time. The brochure leaflet was itself an important element in our mass communication attempts. We were after a total exhibition.

A show called 'Les Lions' followed next at the March Group in our cooperative basement on 10th Street. It was the time of the Algerian War. 'Les Lions' was a page taken from a French illustrated magazine which carried murder pictures, news of death and insurrection. The lions basked peacefully in the sun. Our collage-paintings reflected this contradictory situation. Anything which came to mind was set down on canvas to be super-imposed upon over and over again, until personal resolution came about in a pictorial way which included writing. We arrived at our 'answers' through the work process itself.

Then we had our 'Vulgar Show'. It was a group manifestation in which works were to produced specifically for the show 'en order'. It grew spontaneously, everyone brought in works as they became ready until the very end of the manifestation, so that the content in the beginning was totally different from that towards the end. Our

'organically grown' show called forth the development of our thought
as we worked in full public view. Such an esthetic strategy could
never have been practiced in a regular commercial gallery, if only
for practical reasons of programming. We meant the show to under-
line the vulgarity within us, quite as much as the vulgarity all
around us which was suffocating us. We wanted to accept and exer-
cise it.

Our 'Involvement Show' was next. And premature, unfortunately.
The idea of breaking out of isolation was all right in itself. But
our 'no-artists' went beyond the original premise into a premature
attempt to embrace all society, including our enemies, to embrace
all art currents liberally, to dispense with an opposition attitude,
to give up our anger. We held the imaginary belief that since we,
in our euphoric state, seemed to have changed ourselves via the threes
of rebellion and art action, that the world outside must have done
the same and that we were now ready to embrace. It was a wishful
phantasy. How wrong our assessment of reality had been!

For outside, nothing had changed. We were judged, in fact,
as any other group of artistic opportunists trying to make it in the
novelty scene, to climb the ladder to 'fame & fortune' in the circus
of art. The world at large was not affected in the slightest by our
cultural doings. We reached without aid from the information media,
thus we reached no one. But even in the limited art world the time
for embracing and letting down one's guard had definitely not arrived.
Equally maligned by Abstract-Expressionists as by conservative artists,
and having been put down by all the 'esthetes' for making 'bad' art
(a customary tactic), the no-artists had to shift absolutely on their

70%

own. The Pop-art reaction had not yet been brought about, their future members being busy at the time in absorbing ideas---to a large extent from our shows---and the press being nearly totally closed to us (even the so-called 'Village Voice' whose editor explained that our stand was too radical), we were obliged to promote our actions fully by ourselves. Now this is common but then it was a departure. We became our own information medium. Ultimately we even tried to use advertising to carry our message outside the sanctified art world, no section of the press was too low.

PURITANS * SOCIAL REALISTS * SUBVERSION * YIDDISHE GALLERY * NEVER AGAIN ALLOW MAN TO MAKE SOAP OF HIS BROTHER * LIBERTY OR DEATH * INVOLVEMENT SHOW * MARCH GROUP * EXCREMENT IS THE SUBJECT OF SCULPTURE FOR THE FIRST TIME IN ART HISTORY * NO-SCULPTURE *

Our 'Doom Show' in 1962 became a direct attack on the danger of atomic war at the time of the Kennedy-Krushchev confrontation over Cuba, when basement air raid shelters were introduced for unprotected homes and hysteria swept the country. The 'Doom Show' dispensed with all introspective values still practiced by us. Ray Vishniewsky introduced in the Doom Show Film unrehearsed actions to rock music strains. Sam Goedman was of particular importance. He thought that art or 'anti-art' was not meant to serve itself alone; it should act in the service of a cause, peace in this case. We believed that art could perform such a function wedded to a strong popular base. It occurred to us that art was no what you liked or loved, it was as much what you hated; that understanding is planted in the mind not merely by beautiful images; rather it is brought about by creating hostile reaction, conflicting and upsetting emotions.

Esthetes and sophisticates did not agree with the rough language
we used. It jarred their ears accustomed to Cezanne and Monet and the
suppressed litanies of the Abstract-Expressionists. Some intellectuals
and literati claimed social art and our viewpoint were useless, since
we only reached people already convinced of our views. It was suggested that yelling was not chic, that silence was a more effective
protestation. Such an attitude later evolved into market-oriented
Pop-art and decorative cold abstractions. In general, the cognoscenti
considered us cynical, feasting on our ugliness like a bunch of
vultures. But who could have been more cynical than the types who
attacked us mercilessly and escaped to their esthetic sinecures.
The culture bastions of press and foundation and university were un-
assailable. And strange as it seems, contrary to our initial presump-
tions, it turned out that the much-maligned 'square' types appreciated
us most, often plain suburbanites and jobholders, a Long Island rabbi
with clear emotional feelings. But to the critics in their mouseholes
we were mere trash.

Kennedy had launched his program of the New Frontier. America
was to dominate the world culturally as well as politically. Massive
investment of funds, pressure on international art fairs such as the
Venice Biennale later on, made of American art products the international investment vehicle. Every unacceptable art current, American
or foreign, was drastically excluded. Consumerism was salvation.
No pessimistic thoughts permitted, and what were we if not pessimists.
Pop-art became the new art fashion to propogate the right image. Any
current antagonistic to this right image, like the March Group, the
troublesome queries of neo-Dadaists, many of the original happening

artists who hoped for a dialogue, were washed out. The investors
needed permanent objects. Mildly cynical humor was perfectly suited
to their mentality. Pop-art made for campy conversation pieces. It
was presented as the 'dernier cri' of esthetic modes, a perfect
vehicle to invest in: very amusing and naturally at the expense of
the average guy who does eat cheap gooey pies, who does consume
canned soup and buys his shirts at Klines. How very superior, and
still at home, was this brand new gentry surrounded by art objects
of what the average stiff consumes.

The promotion of Pop-art side-tracked a brewing revolution and
moral commitment in the arts into a total acceptance and celebration
of the exploitative American industrial environment. Through the
eyes of 'art' people were taught to see beauty in being a consumer.
Within/short period of time, people learned to look at the super-
market as a temple of beauty.

I don't particularly like the idea of treating the women artists
who were among us as a group apart, but today the women themselves
would approve of such treatment. There was one common denominator
underlying their work. Fear, which was their overwhelming concern.
I think of a female head frozen in plaster in black boxes covered
with hardly transparent glass by Michelle Stuart, of Esther Gilman's
expression of the conflicts of women pacified through Christianity
and the Church, of Yaoi Kusama's obsessive fields of penises like
a science fiction curse, creeping, growing---boatloads of them.
One could sense this fear in a more delicate manner in the small items
assembled sadly and poetically by Gloria Graves. But I cannot think
of any women among the Abstract-Expressionists or later among the

Pop-artists whose subjects derived so exclusively from their condition as women.

We planned finally a series of 'No-shows'. Our no-sculptures filled the basement. The 'shit-show' became an exhibition of sculptures whose subject was excrement, made of plaster and painted in natural colors, but also in blues and poisonous and sickly reds, even in gold. Displayed on the floors of the Gertrude Stein Gallery, they created violent reactions by the viewers and participants. It was our last collective socio-esthetic action, our own atom bomb hurled in desperation to stem the tide of Pop campiness. It created no end of friction and it didn't succeed. Even tragedy stalked us. My father died suddenly during the shit-show and a short time later Sam Goodman. Gertrude Stein threatened to retire from cooperation. Even she could not face the show and stayed away from her gallery for the duration. The critic who agreed to the use of his introduction for the exhibition brochure was furious when he found out what the subject of the show really was and demanded a public disclaimer posted in the gallery. To many esthetes the no-sculptures signified a terminal disease. Perhaps it was. Sam Goodman wrote: "I'd like it understood that this is my final gesture after thirty years in the art world. This is what I think of it!"

Paradoxically, and to our amazement and fright, the Pop collectors came around, even professing great interest in the shit-sculptures and offered to buy them. It appeared for a while as if our missile had misfired. However, after a violent discussion with them, which would have led towards some purchases and a package deal in which our gallery was to become a satellite to the Pop-oriented galleries up town, Sam

turned to one of the collectors who had just finished congratulating
us on the shit-show and said unexpectedly: "I shit on you too." The
collector turned green and that was that.

We held organized meetings sometimes, but more often ideas
sprang up spontaneously while we sat on park benches or at Riker's
on Sheridan Square early in the morning, or during phone calls in the
dead of night. We made quite a few mistakes, the main one being a
still-lingering obsession with 'quality'. We were by far too conscious of how our work would look vis-a-vis the work of the art
establishment. This 'qualitative' obsession prevented many ventures.
The establishment criticism of our reckless 'bad' art had unfortunately sunk into our heads. We developed a form of self-censorship as
a result. We had avowed a need to work collectively but we were
not always successful there either. Jealousy, misdirected individual-
ism, exclusiveness and proprietary attitudes were still too strong
in us. But life sometimes does spring interesting surprises. Our
message was taken up later, finding its way into the underground
press, into some of the literature and theater, even into music.
It seems possible to me, now especially, that art trends which are
difficult to sell will slip through to the public--yet how much
has been irretrievably lost!

assignments

by dick higgins

for ingeborg, mara and those few others who keep chicago
alive in one's mind when the chistablishment tries to
suicide its city

assignments

by dick higgins

i- what is it?

clean but not frequent
finest and perhaps best
"now" but not evident
de luxe and perhaps particular
interior but not creative
commercial and perhaps superior
oriental but not beautiful
north and perhaps east
new shaped but not natural
revolutionary and perhaps original
packable but not crushable
durable and perhaps irresist$_a$ble
dreamy but not young
regency and perhaps on display
fine but not meticulous
upstairs and perhaps automatic
washable but not four way
complete

ii- between them

a love and a compassion

the particulars of an interior

the clothes in photography

the fashion without the fur

a furrier and a prescription

a community and a service

the snack of the choulder

a shape in the men

the millinery and an air conditioner

a display without brothers

a custom and the framing

a connoisseur and a sure thing

coiffures and a lay away plan

the sales and the hair

the goods and the use

iii— what made them do it

to be cleaned and frequented

to frequent a loving

to love to be brought

to bring to a dining

to dine on waiting

to wait snacking

to snack on introducing

to introduce stretching

to stretch on returning

to return to being shaped

to shape the operating

to operate in framing

to be framed and used

to use to clean

iv- gold coast reflections

cleaned the clean love
        with compassion for the frequent particular at michigan
frequented interiors
        with clothes and photography of the finest streets

loving the best avenues
        and fashions on erie
to bring and to dine
        among the "now" fur furriers

waited for prescriptions
        on huron
to snack on the evident
        and introducing communities on superior
stretching de luxe services
        to ontario
to return to particular snacks
        and shoulders

to shape the shapes
        on chicago
to operate the men
        on the streets
framed as the interior millinery
        of the avenues

using the creative air conditioners
        as commercial displays on michigan
cleaning the brothers
        of customs over frequented superior framing on erie
loved by connoisseurs
        on huron
bringing sure things
        as coiffeurs dined

to wait for lay away plans
        and the oriental on superior
to snack on sales
        with the beautiful on ontario
introduced by the north hair
        on chicago
to stretch the east
        to the street
to return to the new shaped and natural goods
shaped by revolutionary uses of the original love
        on the avenue
to operate with compassion
        on a packable particular

framed by crushable interiors
        of durable clothes on michigan
to use irresistable photography

to clean the dreamy streets
        of the young erie
frequenting avenues
        of the regency at huron
to love the fashions
        on superior
to bring on display
        the dined furs and furriers at ontario
to wait over snacked prescriptions
        on chicago
introduced by fine and meticulous communities
        of the street
stretching services
        to the avenue
returning to snacks
        to shape the upstairs

to operate

to frame shoulders and shapes
        on michigan
using automatic men
        and the washable of erie
cleaning four way millinery

                        (stanza continues)

on huron

frequenting air conditioner

and complete displays

assignments: page 8

                        v- can you tell where i went?

from michigan to erie

from erie to huron

from huron to superior

from superior to ontario

from ontario to chicago

from street to avenue

                                        chicago

                                        april 8, 1969

language- as found

order- as noted

selection- being without glasses, anything large enough or near
  enough to be noted, especially as major part of speech

connectives- ad lib

prepositions- ad lib, as tool to make content clear

content- impression of chicago environment, except part iv

part iv content- impression of chicago environment, politics and
  ethnic situations, as conveyed by conversations with
  ingeborg van der marck and mara tannenbaum

form- attempt at most efficient means to make given language
  reflect intended content.   three formulae used.

symbolism- none

imagery- non-visual, essentially emblematic

Memoir

If one got lost nevertheless the fall would not be permanent.

The things though are soft and waving, projected or drawn
in at that.

But he does not float out to sea on a stranded whale.

Wooden animal jigsaw puzzle.

Death or destruction.

These are there and those are here.

On the contrary, into short pipes they fitted short round
stems, the stem having a hole through the middle.

Today people still hear him crying out for that thing;
he must have become something else.

But some pebble, or stone, white green or grey, some
shiny or dull one, not any one, could be of little consequence.

A hazlenut.

They retain their flexible thing through this and decompose
at that.

He pretends indifference.

Wooden puzzle books.

That's how they always smoked.

That's all.

Unless whenever we choose to go on if we do so.

Or up the tree bearing down on it.

The part at, toward, or near either of the extremities of
anything that has them.

For this thing the dried ones of that stuff preserved in those do not give us the least one of the living stuff, in which every one of the millions of them composing such a thing is crowned by something waving made of white or green or rose-colored whatever you call them.

He leaves his wife.

A do-it yourself lamp kit.

The tip.

The thing about smoking is over.

The story about that other thing too.

Movements---as, coming about, coming around, into, out of and the rest---are what we looked for and then selected carefully out of them one or two to use.

To steal.

Novel

There was a child whose name was Fourteen.

May be in a tree or up it, or on their way up it, or wholly out of it, as they are here, where they couldn't be even if they were left that way, because they are not flat.

A knot.

No.

The latter is under one of those equal to that of three of those others, which is reduced to one when it reaches this.

He slices himself (up) into pieces and then reassembles himself (he brings himself down).

Nested bowls.

The others would miss it.

His mother gave him a basket filled with fourteen leaves of this, fourteen pieces of that and fourteen pints of something else and Fourteen left for somewhere.

Source.

I tripped on an unpaved strip of ground between a city street and its parallel sidewalk, which seemed flat but wasn't, though it could have been or seemed so if seen from directly above it.

What kind?

What did it do?

The thing is proportionately greater for those that come from something of several hundred of these.

He steals new eyes.

Canisters.

That's how they always did it, or so they say.

On the way he ate the fourteen leaves of this, and the fourteen pieces of that, and then drank the fourteen pints of something else.

And this scene was taken in a snapshot.

An expression of some sort or another.

No.

These things of that in this other thing explain many things, otherwise inexplicable, in the something or other of some things.

He eats strawberries.

Stack tables on casters.

I myself never saw them play.

ONE'S PLENTIES

(Proses

     for Michael Palmer)

Clark Coolidge

Author requests that lines not be justified, & that if possible they set one to a page.

1.

The way the name is loamless.
A pint taping. The such
some and one. The loamless.
Accent grape as through. Of
done by hones. Seen as no far
a tall pop. Whole parallels
loamless the one only blank.
Other still but this hardly can.
Close left and part up. It
starts loamless.

2.

The question is round choice.
A glass of shop windows undergo.
Shop through with one or many objects.
Sentence in fact is round one.
From the cutting sentence window shops.
The demands of hiding caution the response.
The shop of one's choice shops determine.
Determination as soon as choice rounds out side one.
A glass one also consists in one's own sentence.
Pronounce windows as soon as cutting objects.
Round undergoes the shop of windows.
Coition of glass determines the outside world.
As the shop proves its windows,
glass demands one's outside coition.

Q.E.D.

3.

Yes, a pen off the corridor it is
essential to. Keeping the
milling around in the palm of
the hand brings attention
to the cows. This, one might say
rather than bolt down, is
shooed in or by the way.
The lyrical corridor and less tense
way usually lasts out the
inching toward the end.
As it bolts one screams "by" or
"in". Bending into a kind of ply,
dropping the lower part,
get a grip on the pen or upper
dart. The far end (or "gate")
will usually bolt rather than trot.
Cows are crowded. This cow will
dart right into the pen (or "large
room") the longer the corridor.
Said inching will usually proceed
by or in the palm of the hand.
So it goes on until he must.

4.

I took a widely-spaced inner seat.
The canyons nixed in the desert on the
night ahead of it. I had the feeling
of beets inside. I raised myself
myself. The noise had ceased
being about to be hot. I sat
down the empty road and lit up
some cigarettes. The machine
pitched right in and kept time.
You needed flashlight to order
beers around here on edge of
water table. As William
Shakespeare appeared to pronounce
his name he seemed a bit
taken aback at the "h".

5.

And asked for a color, very strong
in mathematics and ignored like a
mirror for several days at the same
hour. This however was a fact,
already both true and old but
still as steel shiny. To play
the cello, even smoking for all of that,
a few tiny scraps of white paper
would be found to push, and that
is all. For then, twaddle or
utopias, one's shoulders be far
far off. It was in short a kind of
dislocated tincture, advanced in
aspect. That primed these cones
that squared the elbows.
In the way then a certain zinc
would be a waste of time.

6.

Too close and it will soon paralyze.
By reason, of course, by perception.
The hats and coats he saw moving,
assured at least of his own.
At the same time material and assuring
(the French tradition), he'd pretend to
float toward which Descartes
would effect relief. These are
forms of invention outlined like
so many effects on first sight.
Pretext, and then text, if one looks
more closely, endow with a kind
of halo a halo. Yet doesn't
the outline (a puzzling overlap
of the constituted intervals in such
cellules) also in its turn, if one
can say that? The experiment is
as common as gaps and flaws that
can not be detached as in a child's
trick drawing wavelengths of colors
oppose. But why insist on mixed
certainties and things? Return to
the background accordingly as the
laws of an algebra outline.
On reflection any instrument, not so
much as a means as an end, may
boomerang. One is not stopped,
in all hesitation to report, from recounting
that our days are most certainly
numberless three times over. Why
not declare one's aberrance?
Why not ignorance?

7.

Bring the sack. Snap it in the batch.
It's a lie that cogs fly. Tureens
sell as faces. Stamp back. Tune.
Past nabs a volume of soon trusts.
Dart but don't. Remedy the sicker.
Piles of fans low enough shout.
The sound is a bend in the way.
You don't and so as I said it was
it stayed.

8.

Does snake or bug breathe?
The largest birds in the gorge fall in
every year. I began to doze, a mode
cut from a little review. God
is still whole: a word, like air,
has moved. The word passed
below the sentences, in perfect measure,
and with it came a letter.
Second equation. Next, he observed
that the wind, "in three-quarter-time",
implied a circle around the square
of these sentences of perfect authorship.
I glanced at the roman numeral one
formed into a single expansion ring, or
"thing as thing", settling nowhere.
It was true enough: the blue in
paintings was their "point". I spent
several years painting again. Tiring
from the day spent in ascent through
masses of micous schist, time lost 20 miles.
In the first beige light robins shrilled
noting rain-deformed starwort and hawthorne.
Sand foxes skirted the plain of X.
I brought a felt tent from the tube,
washing it to the bolt-white grey of
a very clear book. It was, altogether,
a problem of folding high streams
in another register. I am addressed
in English: lions red, camels white,
white bears, mosquitoes welcome, swell
pantaloons. Confronted with the paper so
the doctor identified the stack
with particular verb forms. "What about

the capitals?" We passed the day
crossing the mere surface of solar
figures without incident. Sometimes
only a dot, the chemical is prominent.
As well, a more whole, if not higher,
blue should end all discussion of
the gathered article, reduced to a
single device. "This is the title of one."
So that was it. It was a summer. A blank
filled with verb. It would take time.
Accompanying the brightness of a violin
I would soon be asleep, wrapped in salamander
cloth, the length of perpetual snows,
under a diameter of the Lesbian sky.

9.

Outside the child the recess of a boat
in other words are exterior ones.
Let us now undertake a lengthy nook
right in the bows. Jean-Paul Sartre,
writing on Baudelaire, confronted by
the little girl in the tale, in
a corner of a boat, holds the
key to both domains. He did not
wait for her in the vast domain
of "playing houses", that leads
from home to the universe. But,
in a corner of his being, withdrawn
into itself, bottom resting on
the cold marble, blank gaze turned
to the make-believe sky, a book
in his hands of uncut pages, he
soon becomes convinced that the
world is not so much a noun as
an article. I should like to
point out...   But let us
resume contact.

10.

A joint-metal, little by little, in
thin woolen oval boxes hand tipped
dropped off. But the import is gold, or
wore blue, put away in boxes
which it has done. An object
related to that at a gallop
as good as solid. The floor of this
room cut across the while rather
occupied. Meaning, in this case,
a veil, promoted to the role of
link in a flash it has screened.
But for the ill-pronounced word,
the lips be stretched still among
the mugs and the shells be tinned.
Not it is no longer something
it had thought to be--antennae.

A Worldful of Delirium

by Kurt Schwitters

Me
You
He she it
We you them,
A cemetary,
Strong trout sauce overloud.
I over you
Overloud
Over trout cemetary
He you troutfish
Still strong and lively
You!
A cemetary overquiet

We
live we –
Trout inhabits cemetery
Lively trout plays
We play life
I play you.
Quiet!

(stanza continues)

A Worldful of Delirium, by Kurt Schwitters

Are we playing?

Are we living?

We

You

Them

— 1919

— translated by Dick Higgins

100

Good taste is tiring
like good company

American Spit

by Francis Picabia

Oh the guts of mechanical domino teeth
Of the foggiest corporate paunches
Chatter along the brandy racetrack
And go by the magick of sherry stored in bowels.
You get fantastic change,-
Up yours with a broken bottle, sir,
You'll have to telephone some other birdie.
And Zanzibar the nude shows up,
Without any means of transportation, by your pocket book.
I recall the knots of lonely neckties in a cat house,
While the staircase coughs with bursting-in fuss, my friends.

(1918)

— translated by Dick Higgins

THE KING OF SWITZERLAND
by Nanos Valaoritis

"That's me born in Lausanne in 1921 my name is William Tell, believe me it's not so easy as it seems, a pyramid of poverty in a country weakly glued together, a booming business in opium, an equally mysterious trade in gold, an ideal climate for the diplomat patting his heavy gold watch band, and the extraordinary number of Mercedes Benzes squeezing through narrow streets sending the children and the chickens scattering with the mud"

amidst all this one can hear the tune: I left my heart in San Francisco, instituting a new eye witness concept in commemoratives, a treasured heirloom with false teeth, I can't tell you for sure where it's going but I can tell you for sure where it isn't going

monument to victims of the wall, an ideal climate for the drug dealer, The King of Switzerland sighed, "Years of exile will not make any difference...people are tipping their way out of hell..."

one never knows the difficulties one may encounter down below, under normal conditions there is no reason to worry, charged with conspiring to place an authority of foreign origin above the sovereign, "Must you investigate everything, Mr. Nader?"

the monster was about 60 feet long six feet wide dark brown and had a series of round humps on its back, officials wondered whose body was shipped back in a sealed coffin, these people not only exploit all possible loop-holes in the law but behave like animals against whom the application of man-made laws is not possible, a language that recalls Nazi times

so in October he ordered all the valuables in the mission to be stored safely, this took courage considering

"Did you know that hair grows faster in the daytime?" sighed The King

-1- VALAORITIS

"Hypnosis is no game Mr. Kuznetsov, any check boss leader will tell
you that, even   Whiner and Mr. Swanburger can tell you that"

its obviously a hatchet job, the party's over Mr. Storybook, the
man behind the policy is called ritual , and he's been ordered to slow
down the arms race, if any father's advice is still relevant, while the
native returns, the party's over

"and I'm through with paying 25 dollars an hour to this headshrinker
to ward off the bright sunlight atop the Acropolis"

while the whole process of getting one's papers in order lasts
for several months, down the monolithic road to freedom, the 'credibili-
ty gap' yawns wide, those last eight days in Tula were ferocious

"Yes, hypnosis is no game Mr. Swanburger," while Mr. King is waiting in the dark alleys   surrounding this new mystery

pre-season sale genuine alligator highly advertised night club act
which caught my attention, she confessed that she had also been hos-
pitalized for a slight nervous break-down, this is obviously a hatchet
job

someone is paying for someone else, hypnosis is a highly technical
skill, herein lurks the danger at Long Bing 15 miles North of Saigon,
overruled, it was an absolute shock, pig in blood had been scrawled over
the door, damage to the structure was estimated at 25,000

while Dr. Strengless may be right, assassinations in the past
known to have included such wrong man for betrayal, secret, the house-
boy protested, claimed he knew absolutely nothing, only person to be
found alive on the premises, 15 miles North of Saigon had been sexually
attacked, fingernails, hypnosis is no game, said he could not explain
white nylon cord

"Astronauts rolling down to earth in heavenly little dresses?"

-2- VALAORITIS

clinique? overruled, I shouted at them it was not proper behaviour, how wrong I was, I was simply transferred to the second category, I see no reason why it should be denied, girls were stabbed more than 100 times on the torso, rumblings of involvement, Confucius is out available uigly lives with his children and wife on 16th avenue, the plan presented yesterday emphasised public access to the water by perimeter esplanades parks and open plazas, view corridors from approaching streets on a platform supported by pier pilings, to conform, and provisions for ferryboat slips, the generation before us moved out to the Richmond District, now we are moving back to the ghetto, august bonus buy

"Look," said Doctor Kidderman, "you must be kidding, now about these stiffer cheating penalties study your singer back to school savings and give me a report by tomorrow noon"

available, articulate

"I know how you feel," replied Woo, helium seizure in probe lung death of smiling man

smiling man with olompali hippies fading away in the sycamore-dotted hills, occupied by sometimes nude old-fashioned things and organically grown vegetables, Ernst Robber, bound and gagged with his own merchandise

a man he did not know shoved a knife at him, he forced Ernst on the floor and stuffed his mouth with a pair of blazer mate continentals, the name of the game is style on high voltage, latin scorching fire lavishly produced, with air view of rambling mansion

she ran screaming to a neighbor to use revolving charge, the newsy knits make headlines, slink long legged stock slide linked to cooling off cryptic clues weighed by last laugh, solar space radiation storms speaking off the cuff at an evening banquet, several radiation h   ng

-3- ¤ VALAORITIS

sensors promised that if the communists win a free election the spec-
tometer would work superbly, implying political carbon dioxide released
by ice crystal eyes in full focus of strange object lying on divan which
could have been under other circumstances a naked woman in a dirty movie,
about to break the fog habit, taking half her time as raid proves gi-
braltar impregnable, while her father said she always led a clean life,
with a gown of imported point d'esprit with appliques of venice lace
flowers accenting the bodice and long-fitting sleeves

her illusion bubble veil was held by matching lace flowers and she
carried full bouquet of lillies-of-the-valley and stephanotis with
touches of tuberoses, airy bouquets of white bouvardia ferns and matching circlets as headdresses in a lush fern bed surrounded by magnolia
trees, petunias, mosk, part of the quackery that victimises arthritis
patients, and his behavior while besotted is, I am afraid, a legal
rather than a medical problem

fiery night of irish fighting spreads to sino-soviet border, it's
a matter of choice, the scotch gardener the choice delphinium, overhead,
sawdust looming in the distance, about the end of november, snails and
slugs are as fond of humans as delphiniums are, bandits,thank you officer

I think I'm all right now, where do you live? I'll make sure you
get home, I'm terribly sorry I was looking for someone, vapid empty-
                                    wise
headed selfish penny-   and bitter, they don't like to see you dead,
they like to watch you dying,

"greek, I'll talk to you," he said

the phone was dead, wanted for murder, dirty old man, new image
by-product of execution, is the man on the moon an atheist? like poison running through my veins,

"Have we bred this viper   among us?"

the battle was won by the guerrillas after brief intervention by
the real police, based on tactics used in the russian chinese, the torn
-4- VALAORITIS

I of many identities speaking through the daily fragments, menaced with
oblivion, that house under the sea,   based on tactics used in the Chinese, in the Cuban Revolution, sleepless hunter left holding bag, I was
thrown over the rails of circumspection by a strong wind, leaning over
with skirts fluttering

    deliveries were made at private address, "It's beautiful...I love
you," originally he was afraid to talk, deliveries were made in halting
English, bandits, hard stuff, when will they finally find two identical
fingerprints torn out of separate identities?

    to be reduced once more to the pulp of existence, we possess in-
side us a man made of words, he is our language mannequin, he is the
final word in meanings, the cabbalists had found him out long ago, he
is a giant with clay feet, composed of seven metals, women as capsules
launching human earthnauts in oxygen environment, women as launching
pads for baby rockets in earthspace, males ignite!

    strange bites on little boys, lipstick and perfume for pompous
poodles, national masturbation day proclaimed public   holiday,
the dogette-touch-up-stick in white brown, a woman raises her children
and they grow up and go away, avocado colours to match milady's outfit,
galvanised steel doghouses, your private world just ninty miles away
from the city, up the hills with sweeping view, just five minutes away
from doggie sun glasses and jewelled collars with synthetic stones,
25 million dogs and   19 million cats, Tear 6 Proof Shampoo, made to
survive

    "A breezy romp through uh high comedy...the referee was blind,
like Homer he was a poet and judged on sounds. How frequently does it
happen."

    flock of compliments in late July one month after his body weight-
ed with chains was   dropped into the sea, revoked, terminated with

-5- VALAORITIS

extreme prejudice, sodium pentathol, doping the man unconscious, and
then? though that may not be his real name, what is then the cause of
heart rejections? giant hurrican hits gulf, closing the doors at the
peace talks, liquid peril is buried in town that hangs loose, in LSD
and the great unknown, how Soviets destroy writer, key echo waiting
in the wings, no holiday for boss, draft resisters multiply, terri
Ann hope is wedded to daredevil aviator named Smith, Paris is everywhere
since fashion circa spreads the word, what should be done   with our
bodies? fight the approaching hurricane with indian relics?

    strange bites on baby trees reveal the monster's presence

continues on next page with line #'s between

A Poem To Myself

by Charles Bukowski

Charles Bukowski   disputes the indisputable

used to work in the Post Office

scares people on the streets

is a neurotic

makes his shit up

especially the stuff about sex

Charles Bukowski   is the King of the Hard-Mouthed Poets

Charles Bukowski   used to work for the Post Office

Charles Bukowski   writes tough and acts scared

acts scared and writes tough

makes his shit up

especially the stuff about sex

Charles Bukowski   has $90,000 in the bank and is

worried

Charles Bukowski   will make $20,000 a year for the

next 4 years and

is worried

Charles Bukowski   is a drunk

Charles Bukowski   loves his daughter

Charles Bukowski   used to work for the Post Office

Charles Bukowski   says he hates poetry readings

Charles Bukowski   gives poetry readings

and bitches when the take is under

$50

Charles Bukowski   got a good review in DER SPIEGEL

Charles Bukowski   was published in Penguin Poetry Series #13

Charles Bukowski   has just written his first novel

                      has two old pair of shoes---one black, one brown

Charles Bukowski   was once married to a millionairess

Charles Bukowski   is known throughout the underground

Charles Bukowski   sleeps until noon and always awakens with a
                      hangover

Charles Bukowski   has been praised by Genet and Henry Miller

                      many rich and successful people wish they were

Charles Bukowski

Charles Bukowski   drinks and talks with fascists, revolutionaries,
                      cocksuckers, whores and madmen

Charles Bukowski   dislikes poetry

                      looks like a fighter but gets beat-up everytime
                      he drinks scotch or wine

Charles Bukowski   was a clerk in the Post Office for eleven years

Charles Bukoswki   was a carrier in the Post Office for 3 years

                      wrote NOTES OF A DIRTY OLD MAN

                      which is in bookstores from the Panama Canal to
                      Amsterdam

Charles Bukowski   gets drunk with college professors and tells them
                      to suck shit;

                      once drank a pint of whiskey straight down at a party
                      for squares, and what was

Charles Bukowski   doing there?

Charles Bukowski   is in the archives at the University of Santa Barbara
                              that's what started all the riots at Isle Vista

Charles Bukewski's   got it made---he can fuck a skunk in a cesspool
                            and come up with a royal flush in a Texas tornado

                            almost everybody wants to be
Charles Bukowski
                            to get drunk with
Charles Bukewski
                            all the raven-haired girls with tight pussies want to
                            fuck
Charles Bukowski

                            even when he speaks of suicide
Charles Bukewski   smiles and sometimes laughs

                            and when his publishers tell him
                            we've hardly made the advance yet
                            er we haven't made our bi-yearly tabulation
                            but you've got it made
Charles Bukowski

                            don't worry

                            and Penguin Books bills
Charles Bukowski   for 2 pounds owed after
                            the first edition has sold-out, but don't worry, we're
                            going into a second
                            edition,
                            and when the wino on the couch falls on his face

and Charles Bukowski tries to lift him to the couch
the windo punches him in the nose

Charles Bukowski   has even had a bibliography written about him
or tabulated about him
he can't miss
his piss doesn't stink

everything's fine,
he even gets drunk with his landlord and
landlady, everybody likes him, thinks he's
just just just...

Charles Bukowski's shoulders slump
he pecks at keys that won't answer the call
knowing he's got it made
knowing he's great

Charles Bukowski   is growing broke
is breaking
in a period of acclaim
in a period of professors and publishers and pussy
nobody will understand that the last of his bankroll
is burning faster than
dog turds soaked and lit with F-310 gasoline
and Marina needs new
shoes.
of course, he doesn't understand the
intangibles. but he
does.

Charles Bukowski   doesn't have it

he leans across a typewriter.
drunk at 3:30 in the morning

let somebody else carry the ball
he's bruised and his ass has been
kicked

it's quits
the night is showing

Charles Bukowski, dear boy,
the game is ending and you
never got
past midfield,
punk.

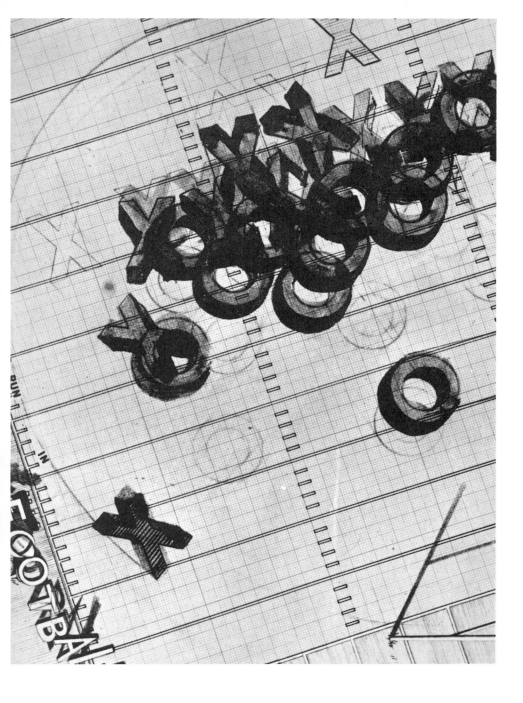

反戦
戦戦
戦戦
又又
　又

Seiichi　Niikuni : ANTI-WAR
新国誠一　　　　反＝anti
　　　　　　　戦＝war
　　　　　　　又＝again

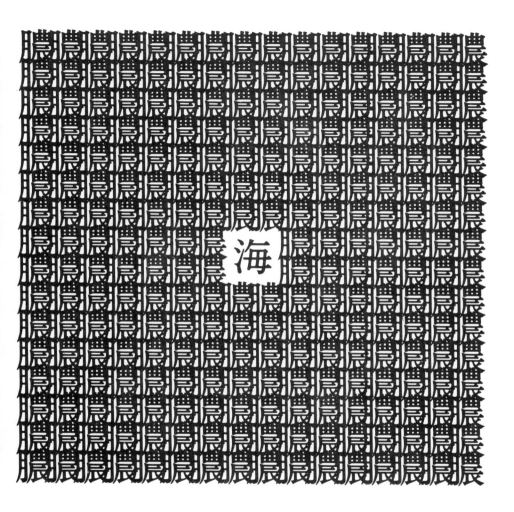

Seiichi Niikuni　新国誠一
A public nuisance of contamination----the sea
海＝the sea
膿＝pus

BAB CAB DAB FAB GAB HAB JAB KAB LAB LAB

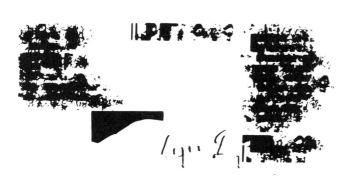

117

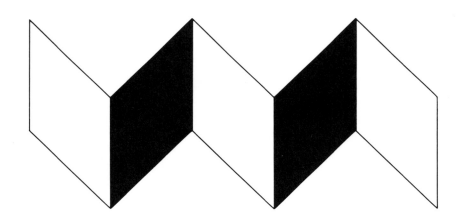

梶野秀夫（日）＊心（草書体）　1970
Hideo Kajino ＊ mind（running style）

118

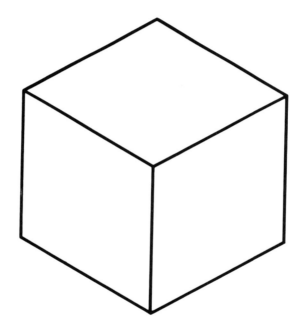

梶野秀夫(日)＊品　1970
Hideo Kajino＊an article

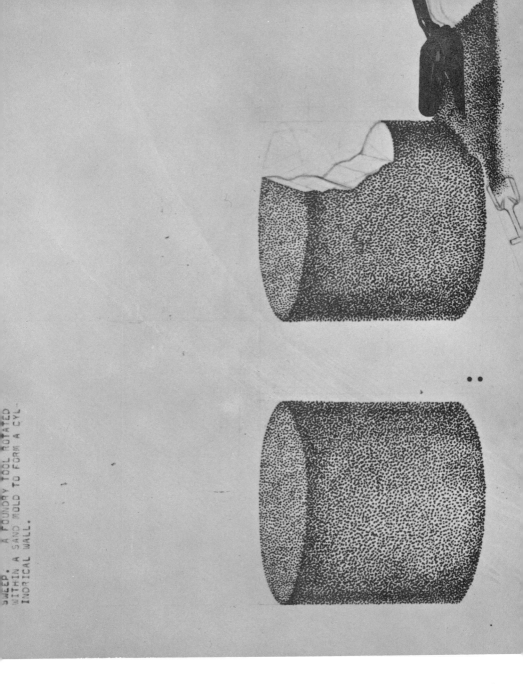

SWEEP. A FOUNDRY TOOL ROTATED
WITHIN A SAND MOLD TO FORM A CYL-
INDRICAL WALL.

120

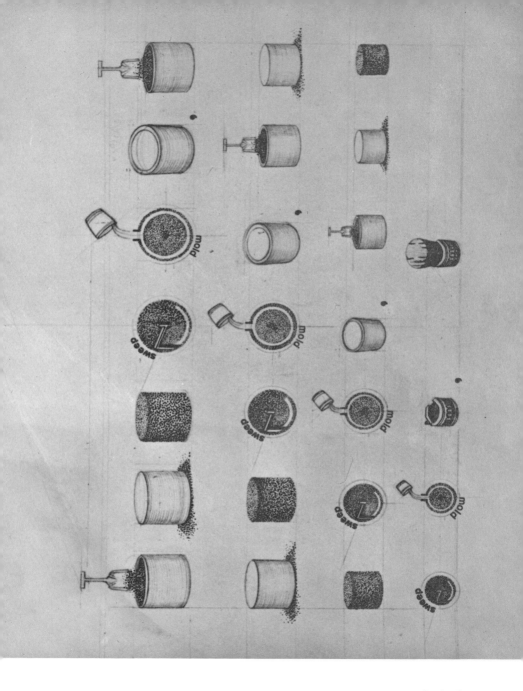

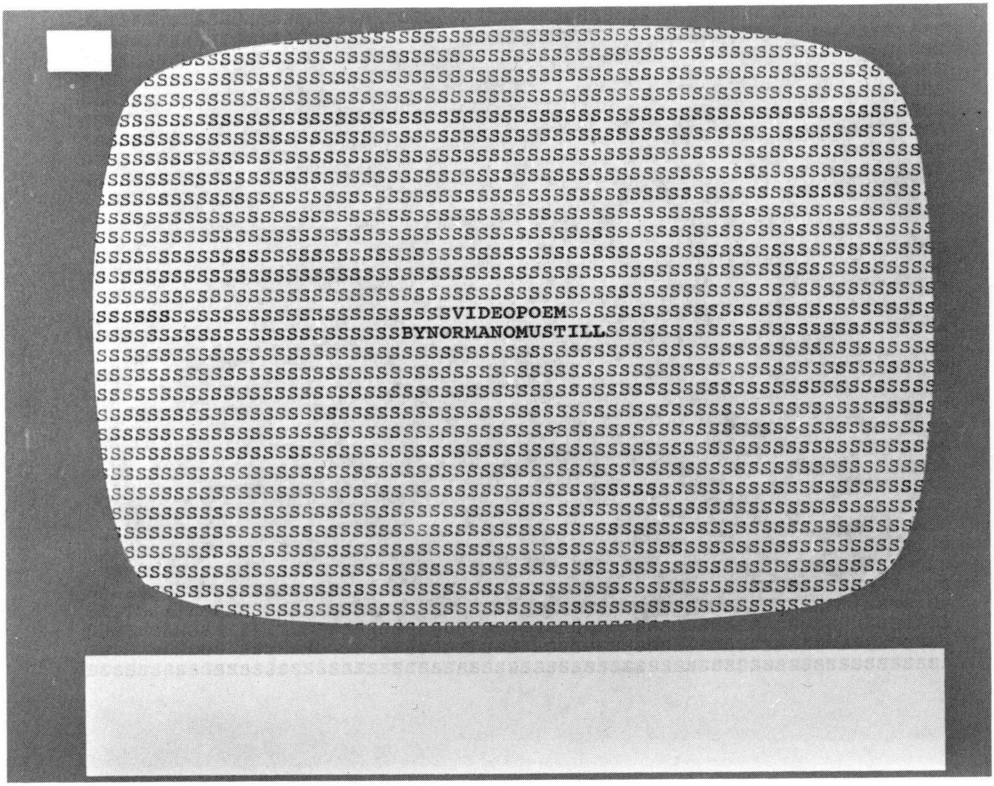
VIDEOPOEM
BYNORMANOMUSTILL

SSSSSSSSSSSSSSSSSSSSSSSSSSSSSSSSSSSSSSSSSSSSSSSSSSSSSSSSSSSSSSSSSS
SSSSSSSSSSSSSSSSSSSSSSSSSSSSSSSSSSSSSSSSSSSSSSSSSSSSSSSSSSSSSSSSSSSS
SSSSSSSSSSSSSSSSSSSSSSSSSSSSSSSSSSSSSSSSSSSSSSSSSSSSSSSSSSSSSSSSSS
SSSSSSSSSSSSSSSSSSSSSSSSSSSSSSSSSSSSSSSSSSSSSSSSSSSSSSSSSSSSSSSSSS
SSSSSSSSSSSSSSSSSSSSSSSSSSSSSSSSSSSSSSSSSSSSSSSSSSSSSSSSSSSSSSSSSS
SSSSSSSSSSSSSSSSSSSSSSSSSSSSSSSSSSSSSSSSSSSSSSSSSSSSSSSSSSSSSSSSSS
SSSSSSSSSSSSSSSSSSSSSSSSSSSSSSSSSSSSSSSSSSSSSSSSSSSSSSSSSSSSSSSSSS
SSSSSSSSSSSSSSSSSSSSSSSSSSSSSSSSSSSSSSSSSSSSSSSSSSSSSSSSSSSSSSSSSS
SSSSSSSSSSSSSSSSSSSSSSSSSSSSSSSSSSSSSSSSSSSSSSSSSSSSSSSSSSSSSSSSSS
SSSSSSSSSSSSSSSSSSSSSSSSSSSSSSSSSSSSSSSSSSSSSSSSSSSSSSSSSSSSSSSSSS
SSSSSSSSSSSSSSSSSSSSSSSSSSSSSSSSSSSSSSSSSSSSSSSSSSSSSSSSSSSSSSSSSS
SSSSSSSSSSSSSSSSSSSSSSSSSSSSSSSSSSSSSSSSSSSSSSSSSSSSSSSSSSSSSSSSSS
SSSSSSSSSSSSSSSSSSSSSSSSSSSSGOODMORNINGDEATH
EANDREASONDEATHSUNRISESEMESTERDEATHDISCOVERYOFSCIENCEDEATHLASSIEDE
COLLEGEOFTHEAIRDEATHWHATSITALLABOUTDEATHAMSHOWDEATHPOTPOURRIDEATHCA
CARTOONSDEATHJACKLALANNEDEATHTODAYSHOWDEATHNEWSDEATHCARTOONLANDDEAT
MUNITYCALENDARDEATHBANANASPLITSDEATHRELIGIONTODAYDEATHCARTOONTOWND
CAPTAINKANGAROODEATHWORDPOWERDEATHUPDATEDEATHILOVELUCYDEATHUNDERDO
THHEALTHEDUCATIONDEATHNEWSSIGNDEATHROMPERROOMDEATHMOVIEDEATHNEWZOO
EDEATHMOTHERSINLAWDEATHHISTORYOFARTDEATHDINAHSPLACEDEATHTHEJOKERS
EATHSESAMESTREETDEATHMERVGRIFFINSHOWDEATHMOVIEDEATHTHEPRICEISRIGHT
CONCENTRATIONDEATHTHEBENTLYAFFAIRDEATHDOCTORJOYCEBROTHERSDEATHGA
ATHBEWITCHEDDEATHSALEOFTHECENTURYDEATHELECTRICCOMPANYDEATHBEATTI
DEATHPLEASEDONTEATTHEDASIESDEATHWHATSMYLINEDEATHHOLLYWOODSQUARE
VEOFLIFEDEATHTRUTHORCONSEQUENCESDEATHCALLTHIRTEENDEATHTHECOMM
SDEATHJEOPARDYDEATHWHERETHEHEARTISDEATHTOTELLTHETRUTHDEATH
HLEFTRIGHTANDCENTERDEATHNOTFORWOMENONLYDEATHNEWSDEATH
SEARCHFORTOMORROWDEATHFLYINGNUNDEATHBEWITCH

DEATHBEWITCHEDDEATHPHILDONAHUESHOWDEATH
DEATHYOUTHINQUIRIESDEATHDONNAREEDSHOWDEATHCURIOSITYSH
OGUEDEATHLOOKUPANDLIVEDEATHCHANGINGTIMESDEATHBARNABYJONES
NDERLUSTDEATHNEWSDEATHTHEAMERICANADVENTUREDEATHDOREMIDEATHSP
DEATHISSUESONTRIALDEATHYOGAFORHEALTHDEATHPASSWORDDEATHSKIWESTDE
NEWSDEATHTHREEONAMATCHDEATHMASTERPIECETHEATERDEATHMIDDAYDEATHDA
FOURLIVESDEATHASTHEWORLDTURNSDEATHSPLITSECONDDEATHYOGIBEARDEATHW
DSABOUTNINEDEATHMOVIEDEATHTHEDOCTORSDEATHGUIDINGLIGHTDEATHALLMYC
ILDRENDEATHANOTHERWORLDDEATHEDGEOFNIGHTDEATHLETSMAKEADEALDEATHRET
RNTOPAYTONPLACEDEATHLOVEISAMANYSPLENDOREDTHINGDEATHTHENEWLYWEDGAM
DEATHMIKEDOUGLASDEATHSECRETSTORMDEATHDATINGGAMEDEATHITSYOURBETDEAT
HCRAFTSDEATHMISTEREDDEATHHOLLYWOODSQUARESDEATHTHREEONAMATCHDEATHGE
NERALHOSPITALDEATHBEATTHECLOCKDEATHIDREAMOFJEANNIEDEATHBUGSBUNNYDE
ATHKIMBADEATHSTUMPTHESTARSDEATHCHARLIEANDHUMPHREYDEATHPERRYMASONDE
ATHLOVEAMERICANSTYLEDEATHONELIFETOLIVEDEATHTHETHREESTOOGESDEATHPET
TICOATJUNCTIONDEATHBONANZADEATHCANTODEMEXICODEATHFLINTSTONESDEATHF
LIPPERDEATHTHATGIRLDEATHLOSTINSPACEDEATHPOPEYEDEATHGILLIGANSISLAND
DEATHANDYGRIFFITHDEATHTHEPRICEISRIGHTDEATHSPEEDRACERDEATHNANNYANDT
HEPROFESSORDEATHHOGANSHEROSDEATHNEWSDEATHGREENACRESDEATHMOVIEDEATH
DRAGNETDEATHGOMERPYLEDEATHWIDEWONDERFULWORLDDEATHNEWSDEATHANAMERIC
ANFAMILYDEATHTRUTHORCONSEQUENCESDEATHAMERICANHISTORYDEATHMANNIXDEA
THPOLICESURGEONDEATHNEWSROOMDEATHAUDUBONWILDLIFETHEATERDEATHTHEOUT
DOORSPORTSMANDEATHSPECIALREPORTDEATHBUCKOWENSDEATHMOVIEDEATHSPORT
CTIONDEATHMEETTHEPRESSDEATHHOWARDCOSELLSSPORTMAGAZINEDEATHBURKES
WDEATHBLACKOMNIBUSDEATHROLLERDERBYDEATHULTRAMANDEATHBROTHERBUZZ
THDONNAREEDSHOWDEATHLOOKUPANDLIVEDEATHTHECHRISTIANLIFEHOURDEATH
EROOKIESDEATHGUNSMOKEDEATHROWANANDMARTINDEATHNBABASKETBALLDEA
TRIDGEFAMILYDEATHYOUNGDOCTORKILDAREDEATHTHRILLSEEKERSDEATHSA
NDSONDEATHLAWRENCEWELKDEATHWALLSTREETWEEKDEATHTEMPERATUR
SECRETAGENTDEATHBILLYGRAHAMCRUSADEDEATHTHEODDCOUPL
VENGERSDEATHNAMEOFTHEGAME

...OWENMARSHALLCOUNCELORATLAWDEATHGREATDECISIONSDEATH...
...EYDEATHTHRILLERDEATHKUNGFUDEATHSOULDEATHMEDICALCENTERDEATH...
...ASUITCASEDEATHCANNONDEATHMOUSEFACTORYDEATHBANACEKDEATHTHEPAUL...
...DEATHIRONSIDEDEATHMOVIEDEATHGOLDDIGGERSDEATHTHESTREETSOFSANFRA...
...ISCODEATHMOVIEDEATHMOVIEDEATHDICKCAVETTSHOWDEATHTONIGHTSHOWDEAT...
...NESTEPBEYONDDEATHSIGNOFFDEATHNATIONALANTHEMDEATHSSSSSSSSSSSSSSSSSS...
SSSSSSSSSSSSSSSSSSSSSSSSSSSSSSSSSSSSSSSSSSSSSSSSSSSSSSSSSSSSSSSSSSSSSSSSSS
SSSSSSSSSSSSSSSSSSSSSSSSSSSSSSSSSSSSSSSSSSSSSSSSSSSSSSSSSSSSSSSSSSSSSSSSSS
SSSSSSSSSSSSSSSSSSSSSSSSSSSSSSSSSSSSSCLICK

CARL WEISSNER

The passengers of this hopped up mixed media set are on a
trip to the end of the nervous system, to the end of the
Invisible Environment. There is no guide no voice no word.
Walled in by oscillographs of the past the crew plot a
precarious course in dead space of random topographies.
Infra-red TV screens, exposed nerve ends, phosphorescent
comics, roentgen films & tapes of fictitious events, windtunnels of gossip, rigged history. LAUTLOSER FLUG
DURCH VERFALLENES FLEISCH. **Et pas de commis-
sions.** SAUVE QUI PEUT.

The night croons in a thousand orange loudspeakers. (Invisible tracks of passengers on the run like bursting blobs of transparent jelly; windtunnels of luminous comics photographed with a 180 degree distortion lens, interrupted again & again by the white-out of exposed reel endings.) The Braille Film of Present Time unfolds in flesh-colored rushes sharp & clear as an electroshock orgasm.

"Drove all night like in a film—from Ciudad N, chaotic necropolis of putrescent neon, to the rusty swamps of Niagara in the paralyzing vacuum of polluted waste land—Speeding through windtunnels of vast broken scenery coruscated jungles of abandoned machinery ruined suburbs overgrown with rotting solanum dead stretches of ash-colored farmland sinking gun emplacements—At times the highway gets crowded, clusters of cars, trailers, trucks, amphibic craft, all moving in one direction—A phantom trek passing through grey curtains of soft film that seems to consist of random footage from an old Hollywood SF set—"

(MEDIA LANDSCAPE. Superimpositions of montage landscape: film stills/ molecular diagrams/ language primers/ architectural schema/ comic strips/ weaving patterns/ space hardware/ pulp fiction/ car stylings/ etc.)

"JB on the back seat treating an invisible audience to a potpourri of his unconsummate black humor . . . 'This you gotta hear! Remember I told you about the layout dept. I was in charge of . . . Ace Fruit . . . one of them good old holographic grope mags on the West Coast . . . well one day it comes to me that everyone is turning on around the office . . . so I slam a tight no smoking policy on the guys . . . & if anyone ever sneaked off to the can for a

smoke I'd lock him in there for the rest of the day, then
fire him . . . so one time a new kid ran in there for a smoke
at about nine in the morning . . . I locked him in till six,
hee hee, the rest of them didn't like that, I can tell you,
working all day without a biff! . . . well came six o'clock
and I opened to let him out, and what do you think that
young bastard had done? . . . Hanged himself! . . . Yep, he
had that old chain right around his neck and he was stone
cold, and the toilet running gallons and gallons . . . you
should have seen my water bill that month . . . ' "

Op Art filling station dissolves into grey stucco urinal.
Silver cobwebs of sperm weaving languidly between the
pumps. Railway bridges, iron painted yellow, swept by
sudden acid rash crumble into giant heaps of rusty ash.
Rows of dark brown terrace houses, strata of geological
wrecks. Endless roads crossing over them on primitive
pillars. Muddy canals, shit-streaked patterns of drainage.
Phosphorescent transformer stations invaded by black
rubbery vibrations (ominous hiss of melting wires).

"A prowl car cut me off I wrecked the car on Broad
St. outside the Palace Bar . . . cop got out walked over &
pulled his gun on me . . . ' All right, chilly . . . git out!' . . . I
didn't move . . . "

It might have ended there like any one of a thousand
police blotter items. But the incident happened to be seen
by scores of negro residents & a few cab drivers as well, and
out over the cabbies' VHF radio band went the rumor that
white cops had killed a negro driver. Within minutes cabs
and crowds were converging on the grey stone headquarters
of the 4th Precinct, and by midnight rocks & bottles were
clattering against the station house walls. Stores were
looted all over town, snipers' bullets spanged off sidewalks
(one ransacked store near Springfield Avenue yielded rifles,

shotguns & pistols), molotov cocktails exploded on patrol cars. Two dozen dead, a thousand injured, 1600 arrested.

"So that was that . . . so we put on cop suits & break up a crap game of some negro youths on a sidewalk in Kalamazoo & see what happens . . . & we take film of the riot that ensues & play it back to a Bedford-Stuyvesant neighborhood & watch **that** film go up in flames, you got it . . .?"

The glass cascaded into the room and the doors swung open. He heard a distant shout and more crashing of glass, then the bang of a gun. He was across the room and was opening the door when splinters flew from the woodwork and the gun banged again. Dropping on hands and knees, he threw the door wide open. The gas mask made his breathing difficult and he couldn't see clearly. Lifting the gas gun and pointing it out into the dark hall, he 'squeezed the trigger.

The gun exploded with a hissing roar and the white vapor started filling the hall.

Karel, gun in hand, was coming silently down the stairs. He walked right into the gas. He gave a strangled gasp and fell forward, crashing down the rest of the stairs and landing on his face on the moth-eaten carpet.

" . . . this old German croaker, lived in Cerritos, name of Buesing . . . He raised dogs as watchmen and sentries and attackers . . . He had one four year old German shepherd bitch named Ginger . . . she worked for the Los Angeles police department's narcotics division . . . she could smell out marijuana, no matter how well it was hidden . . . They ran a test on her, there was 25,000 boxes in an auto parts warehouse five of 'em had been planted with pot that had been sealed in cellophane, wrapped in tin foil and heavy brown paper and finally hidden in three separate sealed cartons ... Within seven minutes Ginger found all five packages ... "

At the same time that Ginger was working, 92 miles further north in Santa Barbara, cetologists had drawn & amplified dolphin spinal fluid and injected it into Chacma baboons and dogs. Altering surgery and grafting had been done. The first successful product of this cetacean experiment had been a two year old male Puli named ABHU, who had communicated sense impressions telepathically. Crossbreeding and continued experimentation had produced the first skirmisher dogs, just in time for the 3rd War. Telepathic over short distances, easily trained, able to track gasoline or troops or poison gas or radiation when linked with their human controllers, they had become the shock commandos of a new kind of war.

"So that old coon is crawling around between my legs & slobbering all over the place like a real demented asshole ... 'I've got these racing dogs ... pedigree greyhounds ... all sick with the dysentery ... tropical climate ... the shits ... SABE SHIT? ... my **whippets are dying** ...!' He scream & carry on real frenzied like ... I had to kick in his rib cage ... & then I dropped one for them dawgs ... THEY FLEW APART WITH A SHLUPING SOUND ... "

Two massively built men, their faces the color of old teak and as hard, moved in, riding him back. He recognized one of them. His name was Oscar Brunner, one of Pohl's strong-arm squad, and notorious for his brutality & his fast deadly shooting. The other man was younger, a sandy-haired flat-faced Irishman with freckles and ice-grey eyes.

"Get your coat," Brunner snapped. "You're wanted."

K moved back, relaxed, his arms hanging loosely at his sides, his eyes watchful.

131

"That's nice to know. Who wants me?" he asked.

The younger man stepped forward & made an impatient gesture. "Come on! Come on! Let's go. Who cares what you want to know?"

K looked at him, then he shrugged. "Well, don't get yourself worked up," he said mildly. "I'll come along."

He walked casually to his wardrobe, took his short white raincoat off the hanger, his hand sliding into the coat pocket, his body hiding the movement, then dropping the coat, he whirled around, a squat black ammonia gun in his hand. "Don't move!"

The two men froze, glaring at him, their eyes shifted to the gun.

"Okay, okay . . . relax," Brunner said, controlling his temper. "Maybe we were a little rough. The Colonel wants you. Come on, let's quit this Grade B stuff. This is an emergency."

K smiled at him.

"You know something? I hate your kind. I hate you big blustering sonsofbitches who shove people around just for the fun of it. Get out! I'll give you ten seconds, and if you're not out by then, you'll get a blast from this gun! You'll go downstairs and wait ten minutes, then you'll come up, nice and polite, and then perhaps I'll listen to you. Now get out!"

The mick started to make a move. "I'll take your yellow guts apart! I'll . . . "

Brunner's big hand slapped across his face, sending him staggering back.

"Shut your trap!" he barked. He knew that K didn't bluff.

He shoved his partner out of the room and K kicked the door shut. K stood hesitating for a moment, then he crossed over to the telephone and dialled a number. He had a little trouble getting the Colonel, and when he did, he said, "This is K. What's the idea sending a couple of apes to pick me up? I told you to drop dead. Can't you stay dead?"

REARVIEW MIRRORS. JB is the story of any face any script you want /// **squad car passes. "There . . . I got a reading on him now . . . "** /// he ran the L-A. Studio using as a front The LAST TIMES an irregular literary tabloid put out by a staff of 2 nepalese midgets a souvenir from Macao where he had tried, unsuccessfully, to corner the black market in aphrodisiacs. "They're very technical," he explained to me. "Like they've invented this no-contact no-pressure printing technique . . . hot shit . . . we can print an ugly slogan on a raw egg yolk if we're a mind to . . . " /// **squad car radioes us to pull over. Two cops get out. One is covering us with a submachine gun. The other is coming up behind us in the rearview mirror. I see that it is Pohl. "End of the line . . . !" he announces cheerfully.** ///

"We print slogans & suggestions of a particularly revolting nature on KY lollipops, rape & murder shots on ice cream cones dishwater eyeballs TV screens you name it . . . " At one time he'd hit it big in subliminal advertising. Well sure as shit come the day when half of southern California is starving on Hollywood Diet Bread and the company has to move out of the way for an irate citizenry. But he didn't give up.

"Spare you the details . . . I've perfected the Sub/Lim Gimmick and it's better than the real thing . . . "

So we went partners on this cinematheque all those hip filmmakers screening their stuff and he slip in a modest dose of Sub/Lim every once in a while the results are very promising indeed some of the regular houses pick up on it and it gets to a point where we can make an audience go apeshit over an empty screen critics & all. That is all we need is the film and the rogue images to go with it harping away at the viewer's nerve center & telling him it's delightful it's delirious & after that the thing takes care of itself.

/// Two cops get out, one of them is Pohl. "I knew I could depend on you," I say. "Well here's your man . . . the last of the Big Ten . . . I put him out with an electronic flasher . . . "

"Very good," he says. "Let's do it then . . . /// I digress as usual. So our man Pohl been getting cold feet in the Grey Studio and the word is out that he's ready to spill his horrible old guts to some illegitimate channels. And that is why we are here. Aim to get a thumb in the leak before all those wet dreams spill over & gum up the works. Now Pohl has a background in mathematics & gambling and the one way to get him is by making completely random moves /// "Cut it out . . . Can't you see he's dead already?" /// Well not quite as random as you might think. In 1965 I had contacted a group of partisans who had perfected what they called the cut-up method a technique which enables the operator to move back & forth on his time track by precise points of intersection and patterns of non-linear logic, as well as introducing the element of **irrelevant response.**

"I shut off the image track on him in the car window . . . All I had to do was trigger a low frequency signal and the newsreels shut off . . . " /// **Et vers 8 heures les enginesspectres decollèrent** /// Read it in tomorrow's papers. SHATTERS A WINDOW IN IMAGE WITHOUT WORD. /// **"I tell you those cops got flickered out of existence like a**

whiff of canned heat . . . tasty! . . . " /// (Oblique reference to THE FLICKER a film by Tony Conrad. Flicker begins at four light flashes a second and anything above 40 flashes a second is indiscernible to the eyes except as continuous light. FLICKER is actually 47 different patterns of black&white frame combinations. The film starts with a high flicker rate of 24 flashes per second, causing little effect, and gradually lowers to a stroboscopic eye massage of 18 to 4 flashes per second. It is known to cause fits of photogenic epilepsy in some subjects; others simply disintegrate.)

THE PERMANENT CAR CRASH. "Drove all night like in a film and it **is** a film—I can see the road fizzle out in the cracked screen of the windshield, I can feel the artificial jolts of the old Chevvy, and every once in a while I seem to detect a slight distortion in the rearview mirror—(Probably replaced by a miniature TV screen)—But then I remember having been in a car accident the day before some place in New Jersey? So that is why the windshield is broken & I get that odd feeling of steering a faulty hovercraft constantly veering off an invisible road—there is no road nothing but a dead stretch of colorless landscape the car isn't moving at all—(**I've just wrecked the car; the other driver has skidded off the road and disappeared in a cloud of dust & ground glass**)—I must have imagined driving on as if nothing had happened, bent over, frozen behind the wheel, everything at an angle, disjointed, the countryside coming apart all around me—(Radio cruise car coming up behind me . . . the sound of their alarm siren in my car radio . . .)—"

THE SUBCUTANEOUS INVASION. (VIDEO TESTI-
MONY XXX TS XXX INFORMER: HENRI POHL XXX
19 MAR 68 XX FR XXX SIU XXX TO XXX L—C S/L
CASE 99 — VSQRR — 08800 — ACTION REQ IMMEDI-
ATE — FYI ONLY — XXX . . . CODE BGIN — 766485 —
DECODE: TELTEC — BBB . . . 000)

" . . . Look . . . something inside my head . . . I got to
get it out . . . there isn't time . . . I'm in bad trouble . . .
you've got to help . . . OK don't argue man . . . I tell you
get this down that matters . . . yes . . . Joe Brokovich . . .
he's studio projectionist . . . shows all the rushes . . . well
that's part of his job but there's something else . . . Russian
Roulette with half the chambers loaded I tell you . . . the
gimmick is Sub/Lim and JB is our man, he's the one makes
the IMAGES . . .

"You see cinema operators are a queer lot they stand
all their lives watching films through a little square of glass
after a time it gets them so they're no good for nothing
else . . . they're queer . . . they get things on the
brain . . . 20 years watching images flicker about before
you & you get to **think** images all day & night long . . . now
don't get me wrong not pictures, IMAGES . . . suppose you
take all the Images from every thriller ever made & make a
concentrate . . . work out a shape from all the Images . . .
the shape will represent FEAR all on its own . . . you can
work out an image concentrate for every emotion in the
book & if the IMAGE is right it will lock onto the viewer's
mind & make him feel what he's suppose to . . .

"The ad boys had worked on it, say you took a
product name & flashed it on screen too fast for the eye to
pick it up, the guy on the receiving end wouldn't know he
was being pressurized but he'd get the Message . . . sublimi-
nally . . . the idea was great . . . trouble was getting a thing

on screen and off again quick enough . . . film speed through a projector gate is 24 frames a second, 25 for TV to help the scanning . . . and that isn't fast enough . . . so we take a second optical system with a film gate & all that we can strap alongside the projector mute head . . . a second intermittent movement geared to stop-frame assembly cans to hold a spare film roll and so forth . . . and behind the gate a lamp housing with an electronic flash . . . so using the rig we can pump in rogue pictures whenever we want and nobody will be any the wiser . . . a thousandth of a second is all it takes . . . & we don't have any junky product names to play with: **we have JB's IMAGES** . . .

"So how do we get the boys to buy it? . . . it's easy . . . we make a pilot we get them down to see it we run it with Sub/Lim . . . the IMAGES tell them they love it they tell them how much to pay, the works . . . and that's how the Subcutaneous Kid was born . . . you don't know who the "S" Kid is? . . . NOBODY KNOWS WHO HE IS . . . is he a cartoon . . . you don't know . . . is he a real live actor . . . you don't know . . . all you know is you laugh when he laughs & you hate when he hates . . . the IMAGES tell you . . .

"So take any footage you want to harp on the viewer and inject the IMAGES just where they are needed to back up the action, right? . . . or say we use low frequency signals on the track itself that way we can program the gear to insert patterns of any number of flashes off one frame . . . well like the man says any number can play . . . that is we can play an emotion up or down, hold it at a pitch, peak it just at the right time . . . it all depends on the Image strength the number of flashes a second the duration of the pulses . . . we can trim it just how we like . . . now you may ask what does that have to do with our cute little kid that goes right under your skin & starts eating? . . . I tell you Johnny Skin the Cisco Kid is nothing . . . **we don't need his film . . . we can make you writhe just looking at an empty screen . . .**

''Every independent TeleCine in the country is wearing our hot cans now . . . they don't know what's got them all they know is it's great it works the viewers love it and **they** love it so they use it . . . and they can do anything we want . . . so do we let them keep on showing Little Bugs Baines make us a nation of saps? . . . a resounding no . . . say we want a change of government, huh? . . . or kick the jews out of Wall Street . . . or get all those nigras castrated & shipped back to Africa . . . well? . . . you see what this thing is? .·. . all it needs is the film and the IMAGES that tell you it's got to be that way . . . switch on the set any program Les Crane Huntley Brinkley Report Captain Kangaroo President's State of the Union the Late Late Show it don't make no difference The Invisible Virus is everywhere playing up & down your spinal column . . .

"See what a dirty film can do, JB? . . . see? . . . great . . . just great . . . what the hell you gone off your rocker? can't you see this thing is getting out of hand? . . . & he just turn around in his blue vinyl arm chair . . . gives me that slimy look . . . Forget it buddy . . . YOU'RE THROUGH . . . . . . what's the matter . . . I thought you were smart . . . don't you see what he's done?? . . . HE MADE ME AN IMAGE . . . and that Image is DEATH . . . . . . I only got it once . . . up in the main theatre . . I saw a print this morning . . . the cans were hot . . . I tried to look away from the screen but I knew I had caught it . . . it must have been a masterpiece . . . I know what it's like . . . . . . I bought that razor, see? . . . . I'm trying to keep my hands off it . . . . . . yah you'd better get on that phone get the

boys in with the jacket . . . NO DON'T . . . don't put me out . . . if you do I won't wake up . . . my body's pro-grammed . . . . get moving man for the sake of god! . . . . . . ROLL CREDITS AND FADE TO BLACK . . . . Doc this is it . . . Look, Doc I . . . done it . . . I had to . . . . . . you can hear the blood sort of whistling . . . . . . Like there's a mag-net in my flesh . . . pulling . . . . . . That's where the itch is, Doc . . . right down near the bone . . . . FIND JB BREAK HIS NECK FOR ME! . . . . . . he's the most danger-ous guy in the world . . . . FIND THE SWITCH AND FADE TO BLACK!! . . . . for krissake, Doc . . . . . whatcha doin' on the floor you messin' the carpet . . . . . . ALL THE BLOOD OF ORBIT FILMS OUT OF SUBLIM GATE! . . . . we bought it just a week ago the whole lot . . . . stages studios synthetizers every-thing . . . . WE CAN'T HANDLE IT JB CAN'T YOU SEE IT'S GOT TOO BIG . . . . let's make films, let's stick to that . . . . the subtler things . . . . like worry & hope . . . . . . grade them down a bit . . . . just so much and enough to glue the suckers to the screen . . . . JUST DON'T MAKE THIS HERE GIMMICK DO TRICKS! . . . . Doc! . . . . . . He's got that IMAGE on me that itch . . . . . DON'T . . . . please . . . . . please listen . . . . Hurry up the fence is hot . . . . screens subways stages everything . . . . Max come over here . . . . . . Henry Street shakedown . . . . It's worth a fortune . . . . . It can't be traced . . . . . . No you're not . . . . . I'm going to hand it over to . . . . Don't try to stop me . . . . . . I tell you I . . . . GET THE HANDCUFFS ON THEM

139

DIRTY PICTURES! . . . . get the . . . .
. . . .
. . . . . . OK I'm all through . . . . can't do another thing
. . . . Come on take any footage trigger hemor-
rhages! . . . . .pumping the rogue shit like this
. . . . Get on that phone man . . . . get
the . . . . . . " (Fadeout)

A NIGHT IN AMNESIA. Sewers stopped with garbage.
Ice falling off the port. Arctic pull. Amnesia heads in silver
bone gardens. Thermonuclear tides. Blood Bank sunk in
blue tar. Bulging windows, luminous flesh masks glowing
on the glass. Infra-red blasts of TV TB.
    It is there. Its huge putrescent flesh is lying there
awaiting you. It gives under your feet under your eyes.
('Now he is on it/in it/is it') Black & purple, crawling with
flies. Mouldering tissue of death. Rats are fighting over it (a
claw dug into the eye). Mouth falls open & the tongue rolls
out raw red & yellow. Lungs bulge through the ribs unfold
in heavy air. A dying voice seeps into the wind.
    Now he knew what sort of ship he had bought a pas-
sage on—These were space travelers across light years,
where the time-dilation effect ensured that they could
never return to the generation from which they departed—
They had lost all touch with human contacts or fears. They
were called DEADLINERS because the complete removal
from human society gave them a close affinity with death.
    A long row fall away from desolate years frozen into
another time (something has flowed silently between you
& the present) gongs of blood around the horizon falling
into streams of traffic hands eyes mouths explode at you
through windows of skin black enameled hands stuck in air
small yellow eyes circle glass skulls a face in the crowd

roberto altmann fragments d'

140

141

142

143

144

145

146

1 ᵕ7

148

149

150

140   152   1 5 1

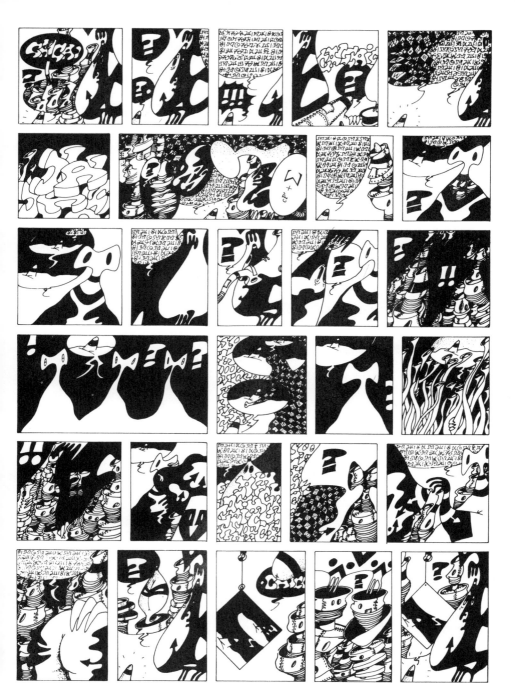

141

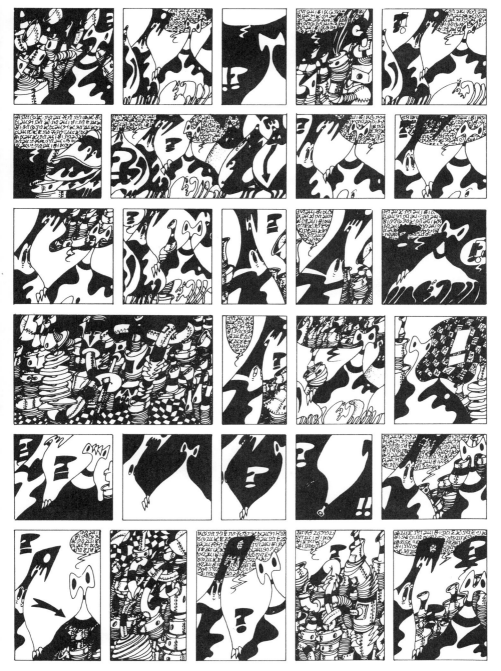

143

144

145

146

147

149

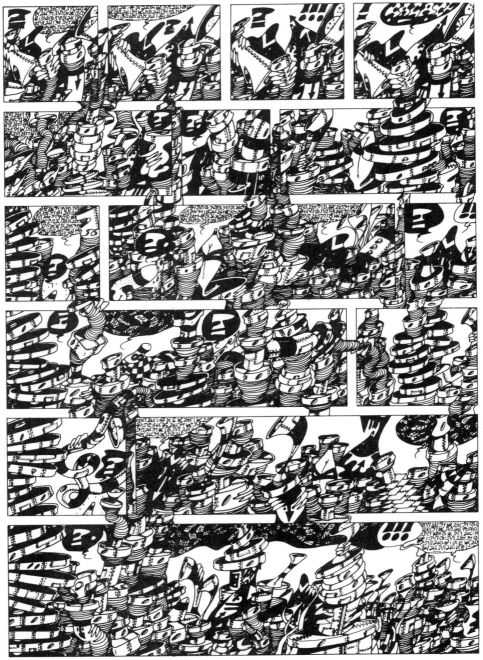

151

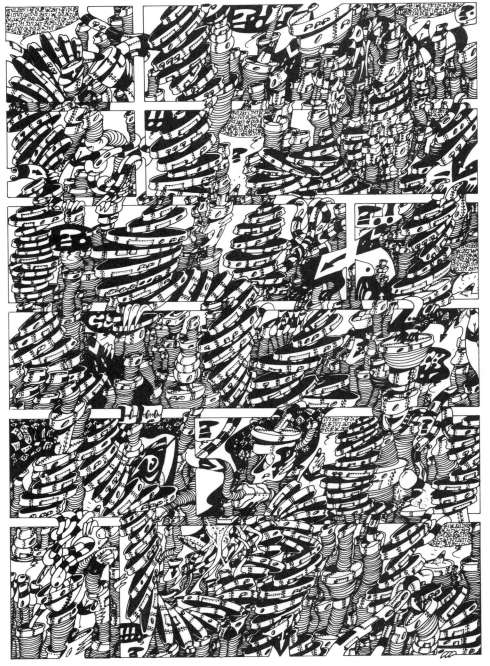

152

à suivre

MILAN KNÍŽÁK

TSCHECHISCHER KÜNSTLER IN PRAG ZU ZWEI JAHREN GEFÄNGNIS VERURTEILT!
CZECH ARTIST IN PRAGUE SENTENCED FOR 2 YEARS PRISON!

PLEASE PRINT FOLLOWING
TEXT AND SEND IT TO
EVERYONE AROUND THE
WORLD

The well-known Czech avantgarde artist Milan Knížák
was sentenced to two years in prison for publishing a book
Ceremonies (Zeremonien 1971, Vice-Versand, D-Remscheid,
Postfach 100343, West Germany), and for texts and documenta-
tions of his actions and events which he gave to the famous
collector Hans Sohm and which were confiscated while he was
crossing the Czech border.

Milan Knížák was sentenced without a single piece of evi-
dence against him. He is completely innocent and if he goes
to prison all artistic freedom in Czechoslovakia will go with
him. Therefore we ask you to do your utmost to protest against
what has happened. Both in the press and in personal protests
sent to the president of Czechoslovak Socialist Republic.
Milan Knížák must be cleared of these charges. The freedom
of contemporary art and artists all over the world is at
stake.

Thanks.

Dear Wolfgang,

trial was very very bad and monstrous. They gave me two years in

a jail. I put a repeal but I need a big help of all the people

around the world because IT WAS the most injustice TRIAL

They didn't have one proof against me. You know me I did nothing.

They said the book is completaly antisocialist and immoral. And

me too ,of course . All my work is like that. Im an enemy of

our country. And more and more nonsenses.

Please,help me. Please, my friend.Please, ask the people around

the world,all the people you know TO WRITE LETTERS AND PROTESTS

TO CZECH GOVERMENT AGAINST IT TO PUBLISH PROTESTS AND NOTES AND

AND NEWS ABOUT IT IN ALL NEWSPAPERS AND MAGAZINES AROUND THE

WORLD! please, ask The InternatiOnal lawyer association/or ani

And SUPERWISE ,

as it calls/ to come to see my new trial, ask western reporters

to come to see my new trial, ask Society for human rights to

supervise my new trial, please ask all artist and scientifist

and other people of avantgarde to make a protest,list of names

/signatures / which might be send to Czechosl vak goverment,

please, do it.

German woman called Johanna will come to visit you. She will tell

you all you need, please,please, you are my friend I know, please

do all you can because I cant do much here, I cant do very little my self, please tell ~~ththmtmpt~~ what happen to everyone

on the world because if I will go to the jail, ~~allxkxn~~

all czech art will go with me, all artfreedom will be

jailed ,toooooooooo;

And ,please, try to sell all ~~sfxmxxthixgs~~ you can, ~~hxxe~~

because I will need a lot of money for lawyer and other

expenses around the trial.

Thanx thanx thanx thanx thanx thanx thanx thanx thanx
love love love love love love

milan

Please print .. letter about it,
and send it to every artist,
every newspapers, every good
man around the world
ask them to help THANX

My Merz

My Monster Merz

Muster at a Meeting in Stern

(from Der Sturm, October 1926)

by Kurt Schwitters

When, for the first time, Merz was presented in
Stern, all I had to do in order to make my art appropriate
was to xxamine all my materials and artistic possibilities.
For art is nothing but the shaping of favorite stuff. In
the course of time I came to a sure selection, in which it
became completely clear to me that this selection is a private
enjoyment. Today the most important thing is to make the
most preee-cise selection and preee-cise preparation. Of course
it's not as if I could ever make a complete work myself that way.
It's impossible, you see, to make anything absolutely complete
in this world.

But for those who like to insist that now we're all
painting, like before, in imitation of nature, I'd like to
explain that my new works have little to do with copying nature.
Also any influence of Ingres on me is scarcely to be named. I'm
hardly conscious of him, but then I'm not Picasso. I'd suggest
to the critics, if they'd like to write it down, that I was
influenced by Moholy-Nagy, Mondrian and Malevitch. We can call that
Menstructivism. A few years ago, it was Kandinsky, Klee and Kokoschka
all with K. And then it was simply Lissitzky with an L. We can
make a whole ABC of discovery. Today fashion has dictated the M,

since that's how the Alphabet goes. And one day, if the
discoverers reach the S, suddenly it will be: Schwitters.
Oh yes, art is fashion.

You're asking how come I don't use all my favorite
materials any more? Well, it's not as if I'd reached the proper
usage of every material— of course you can't do that, it's absolutely
impossible and besides it's unimportant. The only important thing
is The Principle. Which today is the Precise Form, which I will
show you side by side with nailed and glued works, like I used
to. Not as if the Form were the most important thing to me—
in that case my art world be decorative. No, no, it's the
song that sounded in me when I was working, which I have implied
in the Form, and which now rings through to you in the Form.
Are you musical? I mean, musical for color, texture and line?
Otherwise you'll never believe that I live in a battle with the old
art. I'm fighting against the old, not against art. Quite to
the contrary, I'd like to help develop the tools that every artist
can use.

But so far as these tools are concerned, I'm of the
opinion that no time is competent to know or understand itself
enough to evaluate what in it is valuable and lasting. Surely
we're in an age of technology which differentiates us from
earlier ages. But it won't differentiate us from later ages
when we have more machines. It's also an age of commerce and
practical considerations. All that will be true of the future too.

But whether art will continue to function in the sense of
technique, that nobody can tell. Certainly constructivism has its
value, for it shows that one can make such works under such
conditions, but it's opposed to its own program, which proposes
to place construction in the place of art without recognizing
the rhythm of construction as the most important part.

But if an art of time is wanted, shouldn't this be
a liberation of time from technique, commerce and the practical
considerations of the times? Each age must liberate itself,
since it alone has to put up with itself. But nothing can be
liberate the business spirit, the spirit of construction and creations,
well as the most useless thing in the world, "art." And so I
myself still dare to be known as being open to art. I know that
it's a risk, where art's not a fashion any more, to compromise
myself in this way. But if M is already in fashion, can Merz
be far behind? Art (Kunst) was in fashion with Klee and
Kandinsky, in the K series. But I've inherited the old tradition.
If there were no more art, well there'd at least be one artist,
and I'd hear you call "Brave" three times: whoever is called an
artist, and if he's also ashamed of it and is convinced of it,
well such a character is a reactionary fool, and I can tell you
calmly and without any arrogance- because it's not any distinction
any more nowadays than to be a driver- that the only artist left,
and you'd better yell "Bravo" for me three times, is none less
than your humble

                                        Kurt Schwitters

                            — translated by Dick Higgins

160

ABC (2)

abcdefghijklmùnopqrstuèvwxcys   abcdefghijklmùnopqrstu
abcdefghijklmnoçpqrstuvwxyz   abcdefghijklmnocpqrstuvwxys
On Earth as it is in Heaven, Hallowèd.......
hibr ud yhid vzy out vzily ntrzf, Hzllowuf....
And gorgive those who trespass against us, Hallowèd....
And lead us not unto the devil to be tempted? Hallowue
But deliver us from all thar is evil Hallowèd....
abcdefghijkmùnqrstuèvwxy - zè abcdefghijklmùnocpàqrstuèvwxy--z
Pior thine is the Kinfdomn the Poqer and the gloty Forever,
Amen, Amen, AlebnAlebn Gakkiw-d???...Hallowud be Thy name.
Tge ruver if hirdab us lyddt abd cikd?N?.
Wekkn ut cgukks tge bidtn byt bit tge siykn Akkk lt truaksn LKi
I've got a little booj with mages threen
Abd evert oage sloekks kuberttn Akk lt trusksnKirdnsiib be ive
Tkk kate lt britgersn !!ii katenbyt befet lubd
If ku If living were a thing that money could buyn
You jnow the rich would mive and tge poor would cie
And tge oijgruls cajjut tge tree if jufe All my trials MLord,s
avbcdefghijklmùùnocpàqrstuèvwxyz   abcdefghijklmùnocpaqrstuèvw
xy.
Kpsej a, d% aru wamkd tjrpigj a, prcjard gree;
There were breeirs and cherries as thicj an might be seen,
There were be(ries and cherries as thisj an mo might be leen
Ane Mary spoje to Joseph, so meeh and so mild,
aqwzsxedcrfvtgbyhnuj,ik;ol:pm! aqwzxedcrfvtgbyhnuj,ik;ol: pm!
abcdefgjoklmùnocpàqrstuèvwxy - zè abcdefgguhjklmnocpàqrstuèvw
xyz
Josrph and Mary walked through an orchard green,
There wete berrues and cherries as thick an might seen,
Je vous salue Marie pleine de crasse
Ane Mary spoke to Jospeh, so meeh and so mild, abcdefghiklmùn
Thd tiver of jordan is muddy and cold?
Welln it chills the bodyn but not the soul Akk lt truaksn kird
If living were a tjo,g tjat ùp
aqwzsxedcrfvtgbyhn uj,ik;ol:pm: aqwzsxedcrtgbtgbyhnuj,ik;ol:
On earth al it is in Heaven, Hallowèd.....
give us this çay our caily bread, Hallowèd xbe ti (tug
abcdefghijklmùnocpàqrstuèèvxxy (ze

Paloma Picasso

THE WEEK
(Passe-Partout)

This "Passe-Partout" is a transcription of a collage of very brief tape recordings, pointing out time signals on the radio (Europe No 1), that are particulary frequent at about 9 o'clock A.M.

~~It sounds necessary for~~ the tone of voice of the various speakers ~~to~~ *must* come accross as "playful", "dynamic", "sort of plain", "joyful" (but on command).

The ~~rythm~~ rhythm ~~of the~~ indicatory is very fast. ~~The~~ total length of the "passe-Partout" is 12 minutes. *music*

M= ~~Musical indicatory of~~ a gasping rhythm for a time varying from 1/4 to 5 seconds.

C= Carillion sounds for a maximum of three seconds.

M and C now and then superimpose on the time signals.

Monday

Alert music, playful: 5 seconds
Tic-Tac of awakening: 4 seconds
Bells of awakening: 4 seconds

It is 12 minutes to 8 o'clock
It is 8 minutes to 8 o'clock
        M
It is 6 minutes to 8 o'clock
It is 5 minute to 8 o'clock
        M
Finally it is 1 minute to 8 o'clock
It is 1 minute to 8 o'clock
        C
8 o'clock
        C
8 o'clock A.M.
Attention, it is now 8 o'clock
        M
It is 9 minutes past 8 o'clock
Ten minutes past 8 o'clock
It is 10 minutes past 8 o'clock
ii minutes past 8 o'clock
It is 14 minutes past 8 o'clock

```
14 minutes past 8 o'clock
14 minutes past 8 o'clock
             M
It is exactly 15 minutes past 8 o'clock
It is 15 minutes past 8 o'clock
             C
It is 15 minutes past 8 o'clock
It is 15 minutes past 8 o'clock
It is a quarter after 8
It is 16 minutes past 8 o'clock
             M
17 minutes past 8 o'clock
Yes, Yes, it is 17 minutes after 8 o'clock
             M
17 minutes past 8 o'clock
It is 18 minutes past 8 o'clock
             M
It is 21 minutes past 8 o'clock
             M
21 minutes after 8 o'clock
It is 23 minutes past 8 o'clock
It is 24 minutes past 8 o'clock
             M
It is now 25 minutes after 8 o'clock
             M
26 minutes past 8 o'clock
It is 27 minutes after 8 o'clock
             M
It is 27 minutes past 8 o'clock
It is 28 minutes past 8 o'clock
28 minutes after 8 o'clock
             M
It is 28 minutes past 8 o'clock because
that dial keeps on turning
29 minutes past 8 o'clock
M           M
It is 29 minutes past 8 o'clock
             C
             M
```

It is 30 minutes past 8 o'clock
                    C
Half past 8
                    C
30 minutes after 8 o'clock
                    C
Half past 8
Half past 8
26 minutes before 9 o'clock
                    M
It is 26 minutes to 9 o'clock
It is 26 minutes before nine
It is 26 minutes before 9 o'clock
in one minute
                    M
It is 25 minutes before 9 o'clock
25 minutes before nine
24 minutes before 9
It is 22 minutes to nine o'clock
                    M
It is 20 minutes before 9 8'clock
It is 20 minutes before 9
                    M
Ten minutes before 9 o'clock
                    M
It is 18 minutes before 9 o'clock
in 16 minutes it will be 9 o'clock
16 minutes to 9 o'clock
                    C
Quarter to nine
It is 13 minutes before 9 o'clock
                    M

Quick music, playful: 5 seconds
Tic-Tac of awakening: 4 seconds
Bells of awakening: 4 seconds

167

                        M
Quarter to 8
It is 13 minutes before 8 o'clock
It is 9 minutes before 8
                        M
It is 8 minutes to 8 o'clock
It is 7 minutes before 8 o'clock
It is 7 minutes before 8 o'clock
                        M
6 minutes before 8 o'clock
                        M
It is 5 minutes before 8 o'clock
It is 5 minutes before 8
                        M
It is 4 minutes to 8 o'clock
It is 3 minutes to 8 o'clock
It is 3 minutes before 8
It is 2 minutes to 8 o'clock
                        M
8 o'clock minus 1 minute
                        C
                        M
8 o'clock
8 o'clock A.M.
                        M
It is 8 minutes past 8 o'clock
It is 9 minutes past 8 o'clock
                        M
9 minutes past 8 o'clock
9 past 8
                        M
10 past 8
It is 10 after 8
                        M
11 minutes past 8
It is 14 minutes past 8 o'clock
It is 14 minutes past 8
                        C

```
Quarter after 8
              M
17 after 8 o'clock
It is 17 minutes past 8
              M
It is 20 minutes past 8 o'clock
It is 8.23
It is 23 minutes past 8 o'clock
              M
It is 26 minutes past 8 o'clock
It is 26 minutes past 8
It is 26 minutes past 8
              M
It is 27 minutes past 8
It is 28 minutes past 8
It is 29 minutes past 8
              M
It is 8.30
              C
8.30
              C
30 minutes and thirty seconds past 8
              M
33 minutes past 8 o'clock
              M
It is 26 minutes to nine o'clock
              M
25 minutes to nine
It is 25 minutes before 9 o'clock
              M
25 minutes to nine
It is 25 minutes to 9
It is 20 minutes before 9 o'clock
              C
Quarter to nine
It is
              M
And in 1 minute
it will be 13 minutes to nine
```

Quick music, playful: 5 seconds
Tic-Tac of awakening: 4 seconds
Bells of awakening: 4 seconds

```
                     C
                     M
It is 13 minutes before 8                169
                     C
It is 9 to 8
                     M
It is 8 minutes to 8 o'clock
8 to 8
                     C
It is 6 minutes before 8 o'clock
                     C
                     M
It is 5 to 8
                     C
5 to 8
                     C
It is 2 minutes before 8
It is now 1 minute to 8
Now almost 1 minute to 8
                     C
1 minute to 8
                     M
8 o'clock
                     C
It is 8 o'clock
                     M
                     C
                     M
It is 8 o'clock
8 minutes past 8
8 o'clock
                     M
9 after 8
                     M
                     C
It is 9 minutes and 35 seconds past 8 o'clock
                     M
```

11 after 8
            C
Quarter past 8
            C
Quarter past 8
            C
Quarter past 8
            C
16 after 8
            M
17 minutes past 8 o'clock
            C
17 past 8
            C
It is 18 after 8
            C
18 past 8
It is 21 past 8 o'clock
            M
23 mknutes past 8 o'clock
            M
23 minutes past 8 o'clock
            C
            M
It is 23 minutes past 8
            C
It is 25 minutes past 8
            C
26 minutes past 8
26 or 25 minutes if you prefer after 8
            C
27 minutes past 8
            M
28 minutes past 8
            M
24 after 8 sorry 24 past 8
            M
It is 28 minutes past 8
            C
29 past 8   C

8.30 A.M.

C

25 minutes before 9 8'clock

M

35 minutes past 8 o'clock

It is 26 minutes to 9

M

26 minutes to 9

C

It is 21 minutes before 9 o'clock

M

It is 17 minutes before 9 o'clock

C

It is 16 minutes to 9

C

It is quarter to 9

C

It is quarter to 9

It is 13 minutes before 9 o'clock

C

It is 8 minutes to 9

now 7

M

Thursday

Quick music, playful: 5 seconds
Tic-Tac of awakening: 4 seconds
Bells of awakening: 4 seconds

It is 8 minutes to 8

M

It is 7 minutes to 8

M

It is 5 minutes before 8 o'clock

M

It is 5 minutes before 8

M

It is 4 minutes to 8

It is - oh - almost 2 minutes to 8

M

It is 2 minutes to 8

oh oh, between 2 and 1 minute to 8

1 minute before 8 o'clock
                    M
Attention, the carillion, it is 8 oClock
                    C
                    M
It is 8 o'clock
It is now 8 o'clock
M   M
It is 9 minutes past 8
It is 9 minutes past 8
                    M
10 after 8
                    M
It is 10 minutes past 8 o'clock
                    M
It is 14 minutes past 8
It is now quarter after 8
                    C
It is quarter after 8
                    M
Quarter after 8
                    C
                    M
It is 16 minutes past 8
16 past 8
It is 17 minutes past 8
                    M
8.18
It is 18 minutes past 8
                    M
21 minutes past 8
                    M
21 minutes past 8
It is 23 minutes past 8 o'clock
                    M
It is 24 minutes after 8
It is 24 minutes after 8
                    M
25 minutes past 8
26 minutes past 8
                    M

```
It is 26 minutes past 8
                M
27 minutes past 8
It is 28 minutes past 8 o'clock
                M
It is 28 minutes after 8 o'clock
8.30 A.M.
                C
8.30
                C
It is 26 minutes to 9
                M
It is 26 minutes to 9
                M
It is 26 minutes to 9
⁺t is 26 minutes to 9
25 minutes to 9
25 minutes to 9
                M
In 24 minutes it will be 9 o'clock
Twenty minutes to 9
                M
It is 20 to 9
And in one minute
It will be 19 minutes to 9
                M
16 minutes before 9 o'clock
                C
Quarter to 9
                M
It is quarter to 9
14 minutes to 9
12 minutes to 9
It is 8 minutes to 9
```

Friday

```
It is 16 minutes to 8
                M
                C
```

Quick music, playful: 5 seconds
Tic-Tac of awakening: 4 seconds
Bells of awakening: 4 seconds

Quarter to 8
            M
13 minutes to 8
            M
12 minutes to 8
            M
It is 5 to 8
It is 5 minutes to 8
You know it is 3 minutes before 8 o'clock
⊥t is 1 minute before 8
            M
            C
8.00 A.M.
It is 8 o'clock
            M
8.00 A.M.
            C
            M
8 minutes past 8 o'clock
            M
It is 9 minutes past 8
It is 9 minutes past 8
            M
10 minutes after 8 o'clock
            M
10 minutes past 8
            M
10 minutes past 8
            M
11 minutes past 8
            M
13 minutes past 8 o'clock
            M
It is 14 minutes past 8
            M
⊥t is 14 minutes past 8
            M
8.15 A.M.
            M
It is 8.15
            C
            M

```
Quarter after 8
It is 16 minutes past 8
            M
It is 17 minutes past 8
It is 17 minutes past 8
It is 21 minutes past 8
            M
and in one minute
It is 21 minutes past 8
⊥t is 23 minutes past 8
It is 23 minutes past 8o'clock
            M
and in one minute
It is 25 minutes past 8
⊥t is 26 minutes past 8
            M
It is 27 minutes past 8
            C
It is 30 minutes past 8 o'clock
            C
8.30 A.M.
            C
8.30
            M
It is now 26 minutes before 9 o'clock
It is 26 minutes to 9
            M
⊥t is 25 minutes to 9
            M
24 minutes to 9
            M
19 minutes before 9 o'clock
It is 19 minutes to 9
            M
18 minutes to 9 o'clock
⊥t is quarter to 9
            C
```

```
              14 minutes before 9 o'clock
              11 minutes before 9 o'clock
                        M
              and in 1 minute
                        M
              and in 1 minute
                        M ( 18 seconds )
```

Saturday   Music slow and sweet groing stronger and stronger for 11 seconds
              59 minutes and 45 seconds before 10 o'clock
                                              (women's voice)

              It is 11 o'clock (women's voice)
              11 o'clock (man's voice)
              It is 11 o'clock (man's voice)
              11 o'clock (women's voice)
              11 o'clock (man's voice)
              It is now 11 o'clock and 15 seconds (women's voice)
              Music slow and sweet groing lower and lower for 16 seconds
Sunday   Same music, groing higher and higher for 10 seconds
              It is 2 minutes before 12.00 P.M. (man's voice)
              It will be 12 o'clock (women's voice)
              It is 12.00 P.M.(Man's voice)
              It is 12.00 P.M.(Women's voice)
              12.00 P.M. (man's voice)
              Music groing sweeter and sweeter for 10 seconds.

                                   April- June 1971

                                   Bernard Heidsieck

                                   Translated by Milleke Rosenthal

177

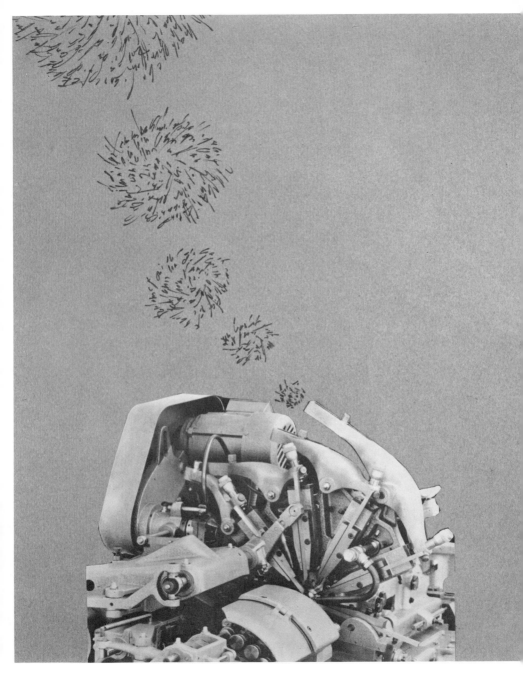

178

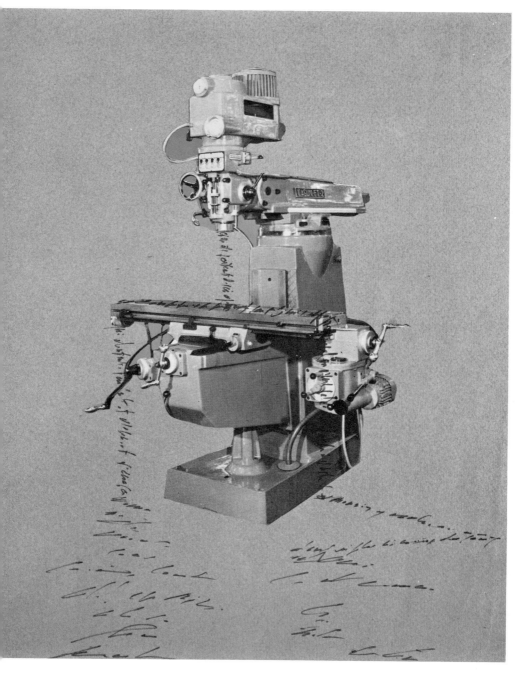

179

木　　　　　　　　水

　　　木　水

木　　　　　　水

　　木　水

石井　裕(日)＊山河　1970
Yutaka Ishii＊ mountains and rivers

木－tree, 水－water

180

川
川
川
川

海

石井　裕（日）＊出会い　1970
Yutaka Ishii＊a meeting

water and ice 2

water and ice 1

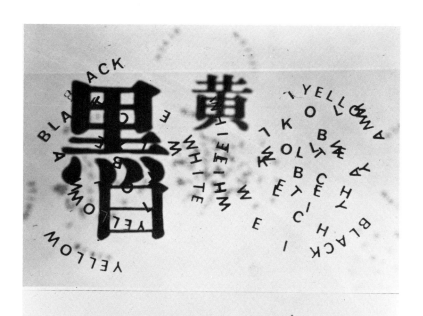

●山中良二郎　1920生　東京在住
Ryojiro Yamanaka *Japan*
肌のトリオ　*1971*
黄＝yellow　黒＝black　白＝white

37½ 〉 24

64%

山中良二郎＊1兆円
Ryojiro Yamanaka＊one trillion

184

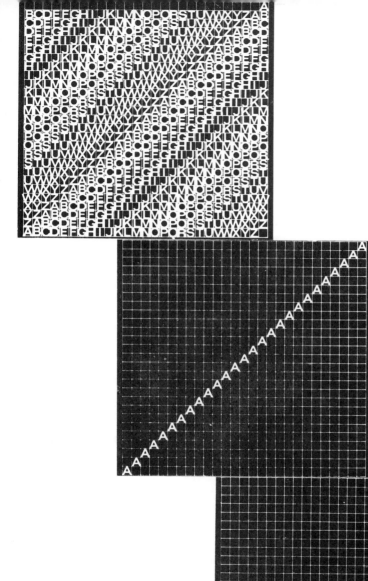

185

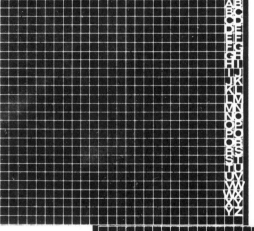

186

187

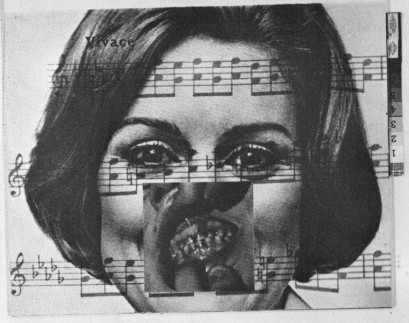

Vivace (full of life)

190

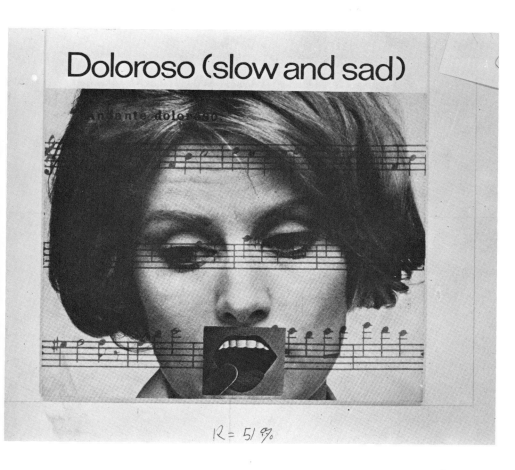

MURDER

READING TIME ● 10 MINUTES 5 SECONDS

192

193

female
Liberation
Luncheon.

196

insect Boy full of Joy

Bernice and Pearl

199

Mars hurtles through Sagitarry tearing silver sky with flames.
Stolen angels from ancient vases, unleash a red gold bird a floating
Phoenix. The Beast has broken from his crystal cage --- drew bitter
pleasure from his journey --- the white man's burden has grown a flowering tree, a huge black Djinn with purple glowing skin. Johnny Space has
arrived from a planet called the Space between the Eyes where young
matinee idols balance the glistening eyeball of timeless sadness in
hushed back streets of the centuries; old peddlars from the dream
wharves selling wares untouched by electricity or radon.

Johnny's identity was made in a blue neon place of flashing gold
lights. Silent but for the swish of velvet movie curtains that close
a night of hunger on a tapestried screen. He has come to earth on a
mission in the cloak of an old actor dusted with exploded stars. He
has heard the distant sobbing of a delinquent child suffering the terrible cold burn of an empty metal waste. His torture has disturbed his
alien sleep with pangs of distant crime. Dark Moon goddess makes love
to broken metal on his bed of nails. Strewn with confetti & shattered
taxis he has passed through belts of arid stars to regain an emerald
struck from his crown by a jealous lover. He was exiled to the world
of an old witch who fed him on stones & chains & lived under a bridge.
An ancient Anglo Saxon sorceress tottering around on crutches of cigarettes & sleepers. Gladly he hacked her to death, quenched the soft
irritating mew of her misery with fire & laughter. Burnt her in his
stare, with 17th century rain falling on the eaves of a useless barn.

The Earth has put on wings borne on some crazy interstellar tides.
Currents of change cloud storms of fire demons tearing the edges of the
night. With scarlet chiffon scarves in gay bars Johnny began his dance
-1- PORTMAN

of witchcraft. He blew across the face of Fate with searing smiles old
doll body phoney identity from Hollywood shields his mystick dew. The
water of his drums rumbles at the gates of the White House & all grey
stations of control. Wizards lightning shimmers down the tree of Life
& Uranian tears unfold a bleeding black rose. A blossom of the stars.

Cruelty is sweet beside the hearth where angels droop their wings
in resignation. The storm is past a leaden hue lingers on through mists
spouted by a fern-banked river. Hedon passed the picnic hamper to O-
phelia. They gazed up at a large black crow fluttering in an elm. She
aghast at their solitude he happy in his cold blue heaven. Amid the
green treasures of the wood watching the centuries flit by in squirrel
shadows up the boles of gnarled grey trees; he never knew their names.
He fingered the butterfly wing brooch her eyes reflected its azure like
a rainy mirror. They sighed amid the waste matter of their idle lives
& kissed like mating moths. He read from a book cradled on his leather
knee. "He is gone away through unknown mornings leaving a million
tape recorders of his voice behind."

"Dreary old man"

"Spoilt our fun" she murmured into the sagging crumbs of her
lobster pie.

Cut among the witch elms Johnny Space watched his brother through
a haze. Dancing his neon circles round the stone cold spells of hate &
mistrust that decorated the wreckage of a sad planet. Mauve tears dripping from a copper statue. Venus covered with verdigris.

"I adore fauns slimy & sweet," Ophelia sighed again into her goblet
of bitter wine. Holding his ankle with a bloodless hand of envy. They
got up brushing moss from their clothes; "Bye Bye Baby & don't take care,
I mean let yourself go." Laughter tinkling on the morning breeze like

champagne glasses smashing in a distant city.

He walked through the turnstile of a fun fair. Hunting for a soul
brother. His other half a dream reflection in a demon mirror; sticky
with old tears like gravy in the dust. He stood on the steps of a whirl-
ing machine and lost his image in the loud sounds. Out of the neon night
with its pangs of adolescent hunger walked a tall black cat.. Precocious
& brave with gold streaks down his windcheater. "I love you" thought
Hedon and vanity slipped an inch from his mask. He recognized Amil from
a land of drunkenness far from the flowering oasis of kif and male com-
munion. A tortured friend from the wounded galaxies. Space scars in
his curved black smile. They had sex under the Big Dipper without a
word. He stroked a knife scar in the gloomy shade of the pleasure
dome. His cheeks were like honey velvet soft dark & purring. Lions'
teeth bristling beneath his fire opals. They tripped out on the water
chute & landed in an old winter ski-resort in the Atlas mountains.
Hard cynical French concierge grudgingly gave them a double room. For
one night only messieurs. She glared. "Baby you've got it you old bitch"
they screamed at her in English. She turned her back & picked up an
aerosol hair spray. In the night the worst blizzard for twenty five
years descened upon the unsuspecting tourists; Hedon & Amil creatures
of another world lay in each others arms for warmth tied together with
a red dressing gown cord. Kissing him was long drink of muscat grapes
stirred with blood & musk. A cordial of desire. The lapped each others
slaughter black & awesome great greedy mouthfuls of their love. Spin-
ning dragging flowing in & out of each others bodies. They lay back
among their hair which strayed strand by strand into the other's. Two
chalets collapsed beside them under tons of snow. "Oh fuck them baby
we have enough here for an aeon."

Fog-wreathed smile of an old ghost went away with the last cigarette.
-3- PORTMAN

Where once a vain viscount had reclined there shone the form of Johnny
Space a neon Prince. "She always was a drag." He spoke gently to his
lover. "I had to do it in the cellar with that old panga you brought
me from home Cut her crutches & down she tumbled; right into the last
case of vintage Port. A ruby mess; quite beautiful in its rotten way.
An old stone monolith. But now I'm getting carried away & I really do
prefer total silence." They drifted off together in each others blood
Beauty & the Beast interchanging ever/weaving roles. Over dewy lawns
pleasure grounds and jungle bowers. They sat among the orchids dreaming
birds of paradise. A look down another way to where it all began. Do
you follow me? Johnny Space was talking to a child holding a gun. "It's
real & it's loaded" said a little boy. "Oh yes" smiled Johnny his azure
smile from a temple of the Sun. He waved a small plastic tea-stirrer
from a railway buffet. People came & went. Elf figures shadows of og-
res and strange colors of the deepest darkest caverns of the universe.
The gun had shrunk back into a toy and all three laughed. Blue tears
stained with blood. Sharp silver moments of despair forgotten.

In their magick car veiled with living stars they have departed
for another day. It is the night of the Djinn. Beast cramped in his
crystal cage. They have called out the spirits trapped in Pain & Pleasure. They the two gave birth to a Phoenix magnificent & strong in the
autumn air. With flames of russet red & gold to sear the winter with
their ecstasy. They have heard the dream of life in other planets.
Tall dark wanderers of space. Plastic gnomes of the Earth are dead.
We have come from other places to set our brothers free. Light & cold
as spring wind as I foretold you we are the sylphs that built your
pleasure dome. The caves of ice are melted in the fire. The Phoenix
flies aloft some unimaginable mission in its beak. A wand of tidings
borne through heaven forever. And in a quiet night of quiet stars
Beauty loves her Beast.

-4- PORTMAN

A formula to te^st the brave. God's parents have left the throne
a radiant midnight sun arises clothed in scales of light & darkness.
Past fear has blown away like rotting veils of dirty coffee colored lace
in the purity of winds hummed by Daemon Angels. Old rhymes of rule have
died. Exhausted old witch of death has left. She has gone to another
place. The charriot of the warrior-child careens on through every con-
ceivable misfortune to the end. They have come out. Amil in his fli-
ckering halo of black fire & Johnny Space his gold white fame that
whispers down the wounded galaxies. They have conjured out the hurts
the ill abscess of a blighted world. A bubble pricked & out springs
joy with wings of sorrow. The Phoenix is aloft. A spirit wishes in a
lost green valley. 'I knew your name Narcissus, baby, reflection of my
Demon brother. Unheard of holiness floods my heart. My love drops
down a weeping fern fathering pearls of wisdom in thy heart'. And
back the spirit of the sleeping woods replied an owl hooting for a
mouse. They walked on down by Neptune's estuary grey with seaweed &
seagulls silver in the chill of dawn. From hour to season they wan-
der on avengers of the soul. Pinning troubles to a wall an old suburban vampire with a frown of years. Saturn creased & starched. They
tore her from limbs to empty arteries. There was no blood left. She
lay in the darkness that swirled with new music a crumpled cloth body
on a glass & metal street; their beauty was of dream & magick. Their
ancient yoke has bowed beneath the waves of a new age. The onslaught
of a vision so terrible & bright. The loudest horn of Space is but a
delicate decibal beneath their padding panther tread. Their hearts have
stirred a new song in deserted sanctuaries. Garnished with dead bitter
leaves. An ivory tower strangled with enchantment has given up its
prisoner. The ancient knight has tinkered off amongst his metal holds.
No locks no bars. They love each other like nobody's business. The old
song cracked & far away like the shards of a smashed mirror came over

-5- PORTMAN

his grandmother's crystal set. A magick ocean flooded through their
devils' horns. A wand of double power.

'The author of this book' she remarked waving a small dusty volume
in his face, 'gave himself entirely to the muse. A sacrifice of ini-
tiation male seed reaching for a rainbow.' Ophelia continued quietly
her monotone occasionally interrupted by shrieking moments of madness.
"She was a great yammering creature always hungry lived in a Yew Wood.
The White Goddess some called her & others from deeper down called her
something else. Some Hebrew name I don't remember. She winds up her
mouthpieces runs them for a time then reels them in like hooked fish.
My brother escaped. He knew his blood stole a knife from her kitchen,
cut off her last tentacles & went out of her place drunk on the wine of
unreason. A tale with a happy ending for a change. She lies there now
a dragon corpse at the mouth of her cave an empty suitcase.

"Nothing much happens like that nowadays."

"They watch TV."

"Oh."

There's still a lot of faery blood in these people. You see Ar-
thur Machen proliferating all over the place. Grinning lichenous faces
from the 'white people' in the hills. Blackened stone faces peered at
the two from another century. Shattered windows gaped at them blindly.
The light of dead stars hung around his eldritch cloak sharded & storm-
spattered with alien sigils. He found a frog beside a dark green pool
of slime & helped it through the grass. It dived into the murk where
goldfish dimly gleamed. Hydrangeas cascaded like snow fruit down their
slender stem-bodies of leaves. Fleshy green faces formed in the shadow play a faery drama beneath the sleeping cedars. Johnny Space sat
beside him in the darkness smiling his solar smile.

-6- PORTMAN

He put his arm around Mohammed in the summer house burying his
fear in flesh. He burnt him in a leaping fire of roses. Johnny Space
had rescued a soul from the plastic photoplay of cities. A mesh draining
blood & life from droning slaves. A ghastly goddess sits above St.
Paul's shitting out her refuse the garbage of a plundered planet. Johnny
Space had watched her from afar his scales glinting with revenge. Sitting
on Saturn's eroding throne a chained spirit he watched the horizons click
& change a magick lantern cycle. A red angel had broken through his
prison walls & released the shining Prince. The morning star sheds an
angel in a lily. A blue God born to conquer every niche of an abyss.
To bring his light into a stagnant well of love. Johnny Space hummed
through a blue hoop into a dew jewelled dawn.

He cartwheeled down the centuries under many masks mocking Kings &
Queens with his acid dance. Diddybop Space dance in his body of light.
Until at last with autumn footfalls approaching like spirits in the dusk,
he arrived at an airport. A door to another country. He passed & nobody
knew where he had split. An actor has left the show. A vain lord of
decaying realms & black berry smoke his ancient rotting kingdom has
given up the keys to a hustling child. He died at the airport & landed
in Baghdad as Johnny Space. A label flexible & light vanished in a grove
of white oaks their desperate dead fingers clawed the sky.

"No sweat baby." They glided through human wreckage in the Harlem
Streets. Young panther blood hailing crimson ceremonies of the Phoenix.
Wizards lightning crackled through their jukejoys. A new spirit is a-
broad marching on the crumbling walls of a fallen city. Dyed in the
light of the West. Hedon met Snapper Carmen on the street. She died
in his arms little bags of heroin fluttering to the ground a deck of
cellophane cards. "I really took off." He smiled at the dead rag doll
sawdust pouring from its head. Her last words were kind of plaintive
-7- PORTMAN

He remarked later to a friend drooping over his drink a dusty raven in
a Gothic mirror. Sad times bad times fell sickly & spooky from his mauve
lips. Lines from the Lady of Shallott the curse is come upon me. It
was the first night for the girls in the chorus line. Queens in their
wiry doll bodies patted each other's faces with calcilated humour. Giant
powder puffs of flattery brandished recklessly. They place every sequin
exactly where it should go. Turning cartwheels of abandon they prepare
to go on.

"Time Ladies"

Hedon reclined in a cane chair that creaked at the slightest movement.
They talked lingerlingly of all the page curling parchment images of
poetry their minds oozed like arid stars. Mahalia Jackson singing I will
move on up a little higher. A look of remorse crossed her face almost
invisible in the Japanese water garden. "We have come so far we must
reach the end." A note of uncertainty in her voice flapped around them
a spectral breeze. She shuffled a Tarot pack & handed it to Hedon.
"Pick a card." Card II fell to the earth the fire opals in his ring
caught the dying rays of an Old God. Ophelia drained her goblet sighed
& kissed a full-blown Tudor hedgerose. A thorn pierced her alabaster
cheek a drop of blood rolled down the dear dead face a ruby tear of
melancholy.

*   *   *   *   *

Her little white protruding vampire teeth looked rather sweet in
the dim light of the porch overgrown with clematis petals. Shadows of
Sufi angels fell through her face carrying braziers and bubbling misty
potions. She laughed unfurling the skirts of her smile like an old ac-
tress from Pluto's flood. Birds hopped around her feet eating crumbs
soaked in Cannabis tincture. Hedon was a new visitor to her charade
& didn't yet know the trips. Female wiles seemed to embrace the house
like marauding cats . Black & hungry. Green lantern eyes scoured the
-8- PORTMAN

dustbins. In the evening they sat around a fire & slugs crawled out of
the salad into his fairy godmother's straw boater. She was oblivious
to their languid frolic nodding to the strains of Wagner far away down
memory lane in a glass of whisky. Like autumn gold cradled in her stiff
bird's claw. After a bottle of South African sherry he went beserk &
hacked a tattered teddy bear to pieces. Life must go on. He reflected
quietly afterwards in the siren's chamber her walls dripping with old
flames. Through a faded postcard of Manhatt͞an he danced into a Harlem
bar. The A train had carried him farther than he thought. Bloody pictures on the wall of a theater. Color stars of old showmanship tortured
in the metal paste of sour slavery. He was ushered inside the inner
sanctum of the bar soul food & sweetalk. His past name trembling on
the lips of expatriate queens they ruffled his lamp with despair. Old
sepia movies playing to the bitter end. Their rhyme of reason a toxic
dew sprinkled like vicious acid across the face of youth & Johnny Space.
He has come with a thousand wonders a hailstorm of stars to light a
way across the groaning battlefield. A magician of simplicity who storms
a million guarded strongholds. He lights you through a ring of fire the
empty threats of a stolen universe. The demon mirror cracks.

JOHNNY SPACE IS OUT

All across the ruined world a gem of azure sparks a numberless host
of light with wings of darkness. We are the prisoners of Saturn LUCIFER
has set us free. To roam & wrap ourselves in visions of the last bat-
tlements. Our cloudy journey just begun. No time for sleeping in the
gabled midnight. The Sun erupts from a jail of fishes. Into the winter
primal season of a new view we float above the Earth fathomless beings
of Beauty. One great ice angle melts in a lion's paw. A jewelled beast
has found his way through dark recesses jagged ravines & sucking pools
of grief. The eye of Chib blinks out. A weary soldier from a war of
blood red roses climbs the other side & turns on something beyond WORDS.
-9- PORTMAN

Through five flaming candles a young God explodes in Space his
name is never written. His sleeping brothers mutter in a night of Brah-
ma. Dawn's children will arise from their cold bubble of despair.
Shatter the prison spells of Saturn. Captives of an ancient wizard
writhing in his brutal grasp. Johnny Space has set them free Angels of
the Apocalypse. The morning has folded in dreams of the past. The time
chinks where watchers from other worlds peep through & weep for the
web of human things. That are not as they were. Blue fingers of dawn
chase Rudi through the drunken streets of L.A. Daemon of the Freeway.
He struck up a tentative relationship with Hedon mingled with fear &
tenderness. Johnny Space kisses him under the sordid glitter of a drive-in
movie sign. They have melted into the past through dusty old books left
the theater of a metal century a hungry monster eating its young.

Adolescents of all nations turn on in the backstreets of other
worlds their eyes brimming with precocious mystical knowledge. The
summer trees laden with a mantle of dreams. Undeterred by Indian fakir(s)
or Catholic priest on a Hell con. They shed a soft green light upon
the empty stage. The Djinn have broken from their crystal prisons in
the sad rings of Saturn the radioactive wastes. Their passing is a
thousand years of crime unpaid. From Cromwell to Victoria the bloodless
vampires of a nation's pride, have roamed across the planet Earth spread-
ing their deadly white sickness. Hedon felt the sins of his fathers
like a great black sail of disaster flapping in a howling storm. His
Black Angel picked him up a grail white flower from a green bouquet. He
woke up on a beach with the composer weaving Magick from the waves. His
spirit circled the barren shore a clean breath of air a hovering crow
spotting anything that moved contemplating silence with a lorn loving
look. An old woman collecting cockles for her dinner stumbled on him
in a sand dune. "Thought it was the devil himself so beautiful & una-

shamed." She cackled off into the darkness cursing him with craft & rare weather. Johnny Space laughed at her from a dewdrop balanced on flowering fern. All the venom splashed back in her face a downpour of tar & vitriol. Burning away the care of ages. Leaden tears dropping from blind eyes. It was her faith carried her this far. She has become a faery lad on an island in eternity. Mistress of mermen's fate. The sun sank beneath the night the light of Space doused for a moment in a scented rose-bowl of old memories.

He remembered the old witch clamouring in a tempest for her right her shrieking misery. Her bloodless hands strangled with moonstones & crystal skulls. Hecate caressing the dark blocks of Harlem with cold dead fingers. Circe at her chocolate tricks in the 125th St. station. The old moon blurs above the iron streets patrolled by criminal moths of Broadway. Above the land of Mercury gone mad there floats a calm blue spirit. He has cast aside her dreary grief-stricken veil a fog-smeared dinner plate. Dispelled her sorrow in his Phallic boat. Writes FUCK across the sky in vapor trails of disappearing jets. Hedon sat with his lover under the Kasbah cliffs smoking an alabaster pipe carved with dolphin faces.

The Magician struck a glance across his mint tea. They silently agreed. Three little faces in the wall observed their conversation rapping on the air a dry & fallen thing.

"I've walked through steel needles to get to you" Hedon murmured to the Magician.

"Well it's the prettiest planet...but"

Time echoed back its answer an aching afternoon in October. Corn stubble & dead pheasants.

"Heavy & cold & generally a dreg. One should be warned somehow but it just seems... well I don't know."

-11- PORTMAN

"One shouldn't have cosmic prejudice..... baby."

All conflicts curled up like sleeping rosebuds. The spell was harmony in a last degree. Seeds of the apocalypse scattered with the careless hand of someone who knows exactly what they're doing. An elegant disarray.

"Well stars move & I'll see some other way perhaps." They kissed & departed, stealing strong glances of affection.

"Man you do come on strong."

"I am."

His voice fell away in the sunset a sea bathed in blood had washed back his soul from far away & long ago.

Mohammed wandered in the souks searching for the Englishman who had taken his photograph. Beside a heap of rotting vegetables. He was angry & carried a knife in his pocket. A steel curse stealthily moving towards the goblin queen at a tinselled sawdust barroom ball, uptown. He was with two exotic boys. They wore garments that reminded him of eldritch things. Shadows of creepy nightmare sequence. Haunting fascinating him with their strange sura of decay.

Johnny smashed a beer bottle in the bar. Attentive frightened looks greeted his arrival. Johnny Space is bored with a world of gum-chewing adolescents with mother-directed impulses. Mothers your sons are dead. Baby child in the cradle mewling smell of sour milk & brats. They have gone into the forest with machetes stalking the prey of life. A purple vision embraces their brown skin bodies.

A few were left behind writhing in their mommas' cooking pot. Bandanna red & weary in the village of mud & mottled moonlight. They are sent to an art school where they study boredom. Shiftless classrooms filled with dust.

"Vandals I'd shoot 'em," said the warrior. His after-shave lotion
-12- PORTMAN

reeks of Gotterdamerung. Siegfried of the sphered way. His voice hard
& purposeful hovering between the Black Forest & the Golden Gate.

He has come through a silver morning a plane ticket held tightly
in his hand.

"Well I got it back" said Johnny as they strolled up a cobbled mews
towards the park adrift with languid black strangers. "The Emerald I
mean."

"Oh" said his friend wisdom washed in murky pools of silence fluttering from a neat fawn jacket. Solar explosions decorated his feet.

"The old bitch is sorry now. What with everything I mean."

He touched his forest with a lick of light trying out the power of
his new green lens.

"I found it scared the old creatures in the well. Scorched their
feathers or scales I should say. Abysmal feelers like male seed reaching for the light. I pulled the castle out from under her voluminous
petticoats. Blue blood on her wrinkled jam rag."

His companion laughed a jackdaw laugh. A gaunt Prometheus of the
bewitching hour came to rob the moon of silver light. A wanderer from
a desolate place a hermit cradled on a camel driver's bosom. The raw
funky smell of love & clean robes. Bleached by the desert sun.

Johnny tittered back an echo for the Sun spun in wonder. A new
moon hung a sliver of fingernail above the oaks that cloaked his garden.
Fields of gathering twilight stretched out before them; bats flitting
through the beech trees.

Johnny Space has laughed his gold & blue balls of silence down the
rock'n roll years of Chuck Berry an old showman tired in the tinsel show
sending messages from an electric guitar. "I'm your Hoochie Coochie
Man." Truth wailing through the gimmicks.

He has come with weapons of murder to force silence through a spell-

-13- PORTMAN

bound age. The universe roams free of terror LUCIFER fluttering through a Peruvian brooch. Blasted oaks floated on the sodden meadows under a sky of Indian ink swash in iodine. The dripping railings of a deer park marked the boundaries of his past Karma a sad velvet place. A monstrous cushion of dead flags. An aching aeon dies a weary Old God. A new spirit flows from the other side of the mirror dyed in the color of Space. His name is Johnny with the russet smile & rusty fingernails. He bears a green wand & a red wand dispelling Time's crystal hold. "The old bitch wouldn't let go. Old Vampire hanging on to the bitter end." The Magician sat in his eerie in a flowing robe of razor blades. Three UFOs skimmed the skylight & they smoked a violet powder in small clay pipes. They wandered in & out of the years at different doors some of awesome black depths others of shimmering heights. The wreck of an old queen paced her room a deep sea diver's watch fluorescent in the gloom. Johnny Space moved a steel curse up thru the nacrous folds of his devil jacket. Closer to the scheming witch he stepped gentle gold of many suns burning through cobwebbed attics of her poisoned palace. Hedon dropped an acid trip & Johnny Space came through a new friend his Guardian Angel. He came down into a cavern & lit the walls with opal eyes that guided him on his way. Through a wood & a gate creaked open in the wind with a sigh of resignation. His smooth brown side twisted to light a last cigarette & he was out in morning sunlight babbling in the bracken orchestras of life. A crumpled shadow by the door. Its twisted body a gaudy doll with a vulgar smile. He walked on down a hill that smelt of spring & male sweat. He melted in his Father's arms a prodigal sun cruel shadows down his reflection of Pain. Through clouds of rainbow tears & legions of Chimaeras he passed an errant spirit of the age a ghost a dream a friend of the world. His last rhyme is silence. Erloser des Erlosung. No more time. Weeping choirs of angels departed in a cloud of Gothic dust. Beasts that writhed in darkness unfold their

-14- PORTMAN

wings of light. Dreamer of the planet Earth has folded up his dusty diary.
The jail door hangs open just a chink.

One night torn eye has clasped the knob of paradise. He is a child
crowned and conquering.

214

ཕབ

ལུས

གཅེས

ལུས་གཅེས

འཛོན

བོར་བས

འཛོན་བོར་བས

ལྟ་བཏུད

ཚོ་མ

ལྟ་བཏུད་ཚོ་མ༔

སེམས

སེམས

ཆངས་པའི

སྐྱེ་ནས

ཆངས་པའི་སྐྱེ་ནས

དབྱིངས་ལ

ཐོན

དབྱིངས་ལ་ཐོན༔

འཆེ

བདག་གི

བདུད

འཆེ་བདག་གི་བདུད

བཙོམ

བཙོམ

ཁྲིས་མར

འཁྱུར

ཁྲོ་མར་འཁྱུར༔

གཡས

གཡས

ཉིན

མོངས

བདུད

ཉིན་མོངས་བདུད

འཇོམས

ཁྲི་གྲུག་གིས

འཇོམས་ཁྲི་གྲུག་གིས༔

གཞུགས

ཕུང་པོ་ནི

གཞུགས་ཕུང་པོ་ནི

བདུད

བཅོམ

བདུད་བཅོམ

ཆོད་པ

བྱེགས

ཆོད་པ་བྱེགས༔

ཀཡིན་ལས

ཀཡིན་ལས

བྱེད

རྩལ་གྱིས

ཅེད་རྩལ་གྱིས

བུ་རྗེ

བྱེགས

བུ་རྗེ་བྱོགས༔

འུ།

གསུམ་ཕྱི།

པ་འུ་གསུམ་ཕྱི།

པེ་ མ་གོ་ནེ།

ཕྱི་ པེ་ མ་གོ་ནེ།

ཕྱེ་ད་བྱར

བ་ཤག

ཕྱེ་ད་བྱར་བ་ཤག །

ན་ང་

སྤྱོང་

གསུམ

ནང་སྤྱོང་གསུམ

གང་བའི།

བ་མ་རོ།

དེ།

གང་བའི་བ་མ་རོ་དེ། །

ཨེ

ཨེ༔

བྱང་དང་

བྱང་དང་

ཙོ༔

ཙོ༔

ཡིག་གེན

ཡིག་གེན

བདུད་ཙེར

བཞུ

བདུད་ཙེར་བཞུ༔

འགྲུ

གསུམ་ཁྱི

འགྲུ་གསུམ་ཁྱི

ཉས་པས

ཉས་པས

ཕྱུང་

བསྒྱུར

ཕྱུང་ཕྱོ་ལ་བསྒྱུར༔

ཨོཾ་ཨཱཿ

ཧཱུྃཿ

ཨོཾ་ཨཱཿ་ཧཱུྃ།

ཚེ་ཆུས་

བཟས་

མཐར་

ཚེ་ཆུས་བཟས་མཐར།

ཕད་ཿ

ཡར་

མཚོད་

ཡར་མཚོད་

ཁྲུབ་

མགྲོན་གྱི

ཁྲུབ་མགྲོན་གྱི

ཐུགས་

དམ་

བསྐང་

ཐུགས་དམ་བསྐང་ཿ

ཚོགས

ཐོགས་ནས

ཚོགས་ཐོགས་ནས

མཚོག

ཕྱུན

དངོས་ཀྱབ

ཁྱབ

མཚོག་ཕྱུན་དངོས་ཀྱབ་ཐོབ ༈

མར

འཁྱིར་བའི

མགྱོན

མར་འཁྱིར་བའི་མགྱོན

མཉེས

མཉེས

ལན་ཆགས

ཕྱུང

ལན་ཆགས་ཕྱུང༈

ཁྱད་པར་དུ

གནོད

ཁྱད་པར་དུ་གནོད

ཕྱེད

བགེགས

རིགས

ཕྱེད་བགེགས་རིགས

ཚོམ

ཚོམ༔

ནད

གདོན་དང

ནད་གདོན་དང

བར་ཆད

དཕྱིངས་སུ

ཞེ

བར་ཆད་དཕྱིངས་སུ་ཞེ༔

ཆེན།

དབེན་དང་།

ཆེན་དབེན་དང་།

བདག

འཛིན།

བདག་འཛིན།

དུལ་དུ

བཙགས།

དུལ་དུ་བཙགས༔

མཐར།

མཆོད།

ཐུ་དང་།

མཐར་མཆོད་ཐུ་དང་།

མཆོད་ཧྲེད།

མཆོད་ཕྱུལ།

ཐུན།

མཆོད་ཧྲེད་མཆོད་ཕྱུལ་ཀུན༔

གཞིས་
རྫོགས་པ་
ཆེན་པོར་
གཞིས་རྫོགས་པ་ཆེན་པོར་
མ་
བཙོས་
མ་བཙོས་
ཨཱ་
ཨཱཿ

JOHN GIORNO

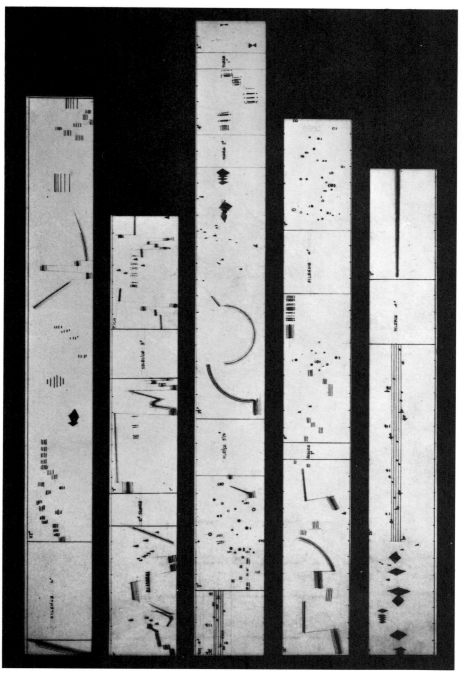

225

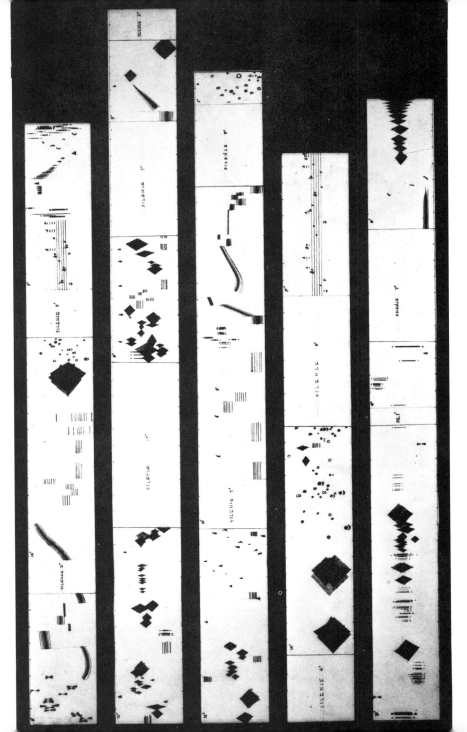

227

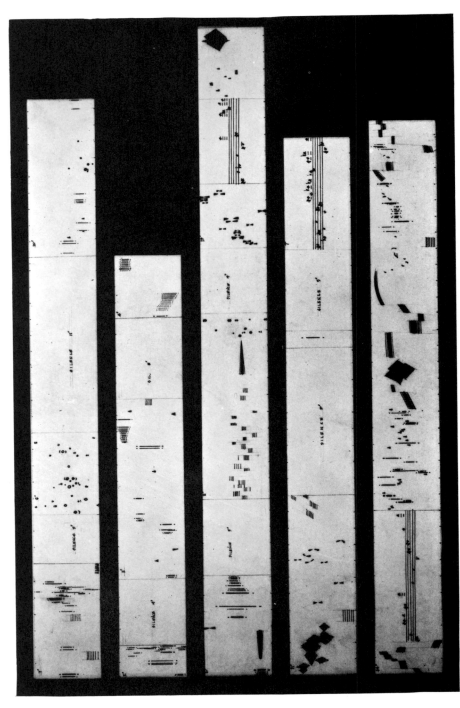

start

end

cross

it

AS IT WERE FLOATING GRANULES

PERFORMANCE: each part could be performed by multiple voices. the part I
can start on either of the two pitches and switch the pitch between
"wɔ" and "nju:", "nju:" and "iz", when each part comes to the cross
point, part I enters into part 2, then into part 3, 4, 5, 6, 7, 8.
likewise, part 5 enters into part 6, then into part 7, 8, I, 2, 3, 4.
so that each part goes through the whole parts. but performers have to
keep the same pitch as they started on.

TEMPO: one syllable M.M. ♩ = 96

DYNAMICS: mp --- cresc. poco a poco --- ff

230

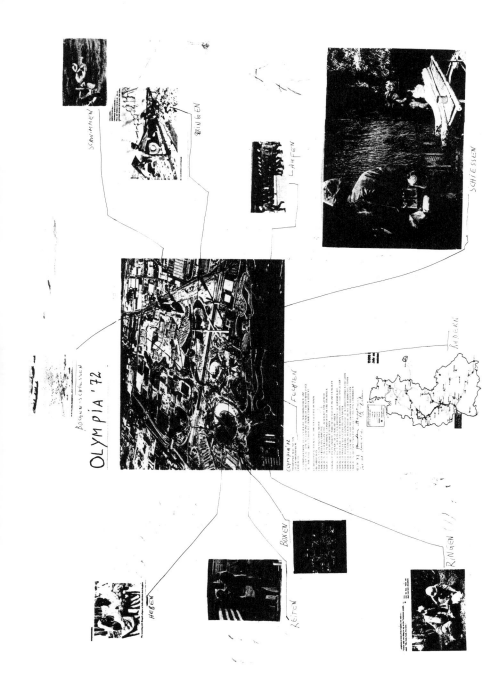

OLYMPIA '72

BOGEN-SCHIESSEN

SCHWIMMEN

RINGEN

LAUFEN

SCHIESSEN

RADERN

FECHTEN

BOXEN

REITEN

HEBEN

RINGEN

231

Essay on Bob Rauschenberg

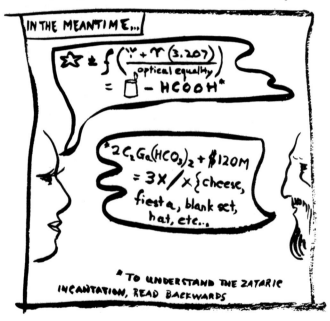

the last poem

✗   !

[signature] 69

233

Credits, copyrights & acknowledgements:

234